Lend Me Your Ears

More Humorous Stories from Roaring Cove

Bruce Stagg

Lend Me Your Ears

More Humorous Stories from Roaring Cove

Bruce Stagg

jesperson
publishing

jesperson publishing

100 Water Street
P. O. Box 2188
St. John's, NL
A1C 6E6

Library and Archives Canada Cataloguing in Publication

Stagg, Bruce, 1952-
    Lend me your ears : more humorous stories from Roaring Cove
Cove / Bruce Stagg.

ISBN 1-894377-17-6
I. Title.
PS8587.T26L45 2005   C813'.54   C2005-903586-2

Editor: Tamara Reynish

Design/Layout:

Cover Art: Reilly Fitzgerald

The Publisher has been given permission to use quotations from the following sources: Page 18 - Permission granted by M. William Krasilovsky. Page 24 - Permission granted by Joan Werblin Stinnett. Page 60 – Lord of the Flies, William Golding, Faber and Faber Ltd.;. Page 85 - By Tennessee Williams, from THE GLASS MENAGERIE, copyright ©1945 by The University of the South and Edwin D. William. Preprinted by permission of New Directions Publishing Corp. Page 105 - Copyright © 1960 by Harper Lee; renewed © 1988 by Harper Lee. Foreword copyright © 1993 by Harper Lee. Reprinted by permission of HarperCollins Publishers.

Bruce Stagg
P.O. Box 25, Hillview, NL A0E 2A0
Tel: (709) 546-2474 • bruce.stagg@nf.sympatico.ca

Printed in Canada.

*This book is dedicated
to the loving memory
of my father, Job Stagg,
who taught me to appreciate
the humour in everyday situations.*

Preface

Since I first introduced readers to the concept of Roaring Cove several years ago, I have been repeatedly asked three questions: Firstly, I am asked about the setting of my stories. Roaring Cove is not a real place as I present it. I was raised in Catalina, on the tip of the Bonavista Peninsula, and just outside the community there is a place called Roaring Cove. It is a spot on the rugged shoreline where a long beach of smoothly eroded stones creates a barachois* between the ocean and a body of fresh water known as Roaring Cove Pond. It is so named because of the guttural, roaring sound made when the beach rocks tumble over each other in a heavy sea. The spot offers little protection from the elements; consequently, no one has ever lived there. I hold a certain affection for this place because, as a youth, I spent many adventurous hours combing the beach and exploring the adjacent cliffs; hence, I borrowed the name for my fictitious town.

Secondly, I am asked about my characters. My characters are based on actual people whom I have encountered, but they are not real; they are representative of the types of people who live in the small communities of Newfoundland, and most likely, small places everywhere. Just as Roaring Cove is a typical community, its characters are also typical. They are neither all good nor all bad – they will sting you with gossip and bring you boilers of soup when a situation warrants it. Anyone who has lived in an outport will identify the likes of Uncle Mark and Aunt Mae, and will know a devilskin,* a sleeveen* and a hypochondriac.

Thirdly, I am repeatedly asked about the validity of my stories. To say that they are true is, in itself, untrue; nevertheless, all have an element of truth. The purpose of my storytelling is threefold. It is to make a soft social commentary, it is to preserve a disappearing culture and language, and it is to emphasize the genuineness of the

---

* A narrow strip of land, often consisting of rounded beach rocks, that separate a fresh water pond from the salt water.
* A mischievous, practical joker.
* A good-for-nothing person who lies and cheats.

humour. Therefore, I start with a basic fact, assign it to an appropriate character, and exaggerate and fabricate the details into a narrative that fulfils my purpose in, what I hope, is an entertaining way.

Table of Contents

Introduction

Roaring Cove has evolved over the years. It is no longer the isolated little town I first saw that day so long ago when I arrived on the coastal steamer to become Roaring Cove's Schoolmaster. Mainland politics and advanced technology have caused Roaring Cove to progress and prosper; or, I suppose it has. The town still clings like a puffin's nest to the high cliffs that shape Roaring Cove Harbour. The large round stones of Roaring Cove Beach still tumble over each other and roar out when the sea is angry, and Manuel's Point still juts into the harbour like a crooked finger. These are the doings of Mother Nature, and she does not take kindly to her work being altered.

Other things, though, have been forever altered. The brightly coloured red, green, yellow and turquoise houses that once decorated the grey cliffs have been wrapped in drab vinyl erasing the vibrance of the place.

The slate-grey fishing stages and sheds, and the lily-white punts* and rodneys* that were tied up to them have disappeared making the once busy landwash look desolate and lonely. We lost them to more efficient, rusty trawlers and to incongruous, smelly fish plants. The trawlers too have since disappeared, and the plants remain in a dilapidated state because their efficiencies were too much for the once vibrant cod fishery.

The coastal boat on which I came, which was the lifeline of the community for so long, has outlived its usefulness and is beached on a rocky shoal and has been left to rot. In its place, a road connects Roaring Cove to Middleville, and to the rest of the world. The idea of the road initially came as an election promise, and it proved to be a good platform for three additional elections before a gravel path was finally laid over Bakeapple Marsh, and the idea of smearing a

---

* A small round bottom boat.
* A small open fishing boat.

veneer of asphalt atop of the gravel was good enough to get six more government members elected. The paved road brought students from all the smaller places up and down the coast. A new, larger school was built on the outskirts of town. Our little two-room school, the one in which we held card games, soup suppers, concerts and weddings, was torn down. The road was welcomed by all, but it denied Roaring Cove the prestigious honour of being isolated, and far too many of our people set out over it and never came back.

Yes, Roaring Cove has evolved, but its people have remained as unchanged as the cliffs themselves. Many have been forced to move away, but regardless of where on this earth they are — and Roaring Covers are everywhere — the blood that pulsates through their veins is Roaring Cove blood. To attempt to purify or mutate it would be like attempting to take the salt from the sea.

As for those who remain, they are the salt itself. They are no better or no worse than people anywhere, but they are the characters about whom I have told stories for all these years, and to me, that makes them special. All have aged, but age erodes only the outside. Uncle Mark White's heart is as big as always, and his opinions are even bigger. Age has mellowed Alfie Lambert, but he is still very much a devilskin. Age, on the other hand, has intensified Aunt Daisy Snelgrove's ailments, and she is more of a hypochondriac than she ever was.

Jonas Pickett is still a sleeveen and Sam Whiffen is still a businessman — shrewd, but not miserable. Dr. Templeman has never stopped fixing our bodies and Reverend King continues to fix our souls.

Old Jack, the community dog, is still with us; he is much less playful but just as loveable and loyal.

As for Thumb-On-Wrench, Paddy Whalen, Walt Churchill, Aunt Mae, Albert Hicks, Winse, and Elsie Hillard, and the rest of the Roaring Cove crowd, they are the very essence of the place, and when they are gone, others will take their place, and it will continue to be the same as it has been for five hundred years.

Medical Mystery

"Water, water, every where Nor any drop to drink."
Samuel Taylor Coleridge — *The Rime of the Ancient Mariner*

One of the biggest medical mysteries in Roaring Cove was not solved by Dr. Templeman or by any medical person. It was none other than Uncle Mark White who cured Jobie Rodger's wife and two children of a mysterious ailment.

Uncle Mark, the oldest and most respected man in Roaring Cove, is well known for his wisdom and wizardry. Whenever the community is in need of a masterful opinion, it is to Uncle Mark it turns. It is he who attends to all matters that require an ambience of magic or sorcery, and, over the years, he has put away thousands of warts by means of a secret charm. Any man, woman or child, who becomes inflicted with these horrible, seedy growths, will contact Uncle Mark with the details of the infliction and within days, one by one, the warts will disappear. Besides putting away warts, he can charm away toothaches and sore eyes, and cause blood to coagulate if a person is haemorrhaging. And, no one in Roaring Cove would consider digging a well without engaging his dowsing talents. Gripping a forked alder branch in both hands and holding it out in front of him, he scans the area to be dug until the alder branch twists and bends in his hands. This tells him the location of the water and how far underground it is. Uncle Mark also has other talents. He knows things for no particular reason. We can always count on him to give an accurate weather forecast, or to predict the outcome of a fishing season. If someone becomes lost at sea or in the woods, Uncle Mark knows where to look. In a horrific windstorm a few years ago I, being a naive Schoolmaster and inexperienced mariner, ran my punt upon a sunken shoal and snapped off the shaft of the outboard motor. My little boat was swept ashore and helplessly smashed against the rocky shoreline; I was thrown into the furious water and washed upon the "birdgage," a splinter of partially submerged rock. There I waited, with ribs fractured, for the sea to claim me. Luckily though, when I was reported overdue, Uncle Mark intuitively knew where I was and came with a rescue team.

Other than his mysticism, Uncle Mark is renowned for his thoughtfulness. As his name suggests, he is an esteemed Uncle to all in Roaring Cove. If anyone is in need, Uncle Mark is inevitably there to offer a helping hand. And, strangers are lucky if they can pass his door without being invited in for a cup of tea. It is this quality that brought him to visit Jobie Rodgers and to stumble on the cause of the illness that had been plaguing Jobie's family for months.

I first noticed something peculiar about the Rodgers' children the first few days back to school after the summer break. They were routinely late for morning classes, claiming that their mother had overslept and had not called them in time for the first bell. I also noticed that upon arriving at school they were giddy and talkative, and they frequently babbled incoherently. Now usually, Jobie's two daughters, Sally and Betty Lou were quiet and mannerly children, but when I reprimanded them for being late, Betty Lou, the younger of the two, shot back a saucy remark. This was indeed out of character and caused me some concern. My worry grew when I noticed that the girls did not look at all well. They often appeared flushed in the face and, although hyperactive and energetic when arriving at school, by recess time, they often fell asleep at their desks. On one occasion I noticed Sally, the older girl, become faint and stumble into the locker room door on her way to the drinking fountain. I took it upon myself to contact Dr. Templeman and officially register my consternation.

Although professional about patient confidentiality, Dr. Templeman confided in me that he had been treating the youngsters' mother, Margaret, for some mysterious illness, but was unaware that the children were also showing symptoms. This caused the doctor to fear that the disease may be contagious and spread throughout the school. He recommended that I suggest to the girls that they stay home until he could make a firm diagnosis.

This I did. My actions promptly brought a visit from Jobie.

"I don't know what to do, Schoolmaster," he admitted. "I'm fearful for Margaret. She's not a well woman. She's forever complaining about being stomach sick and having a headache. When she's not staggering around with dizzy spells, she's running to the toilet with diarrhoea."

Jobie was intent on making a full confession, and so he continued.

"And what is worse, Schoolmaster, is that Margaret has had a complete change in personality. She has no interest in doing anything. She simply lets the dishes build up in the sink, and she hasn't cooked a meal in weeks."

"That doesn't sound at all like the Margaret I know," I added.

"Exactly," Jobie commented. "And she has mood swings also. One minute she may be as happy as a lark and the next as cantankerous as Jonas Pickett. Sure, I came in the house the other morning and there she was, singing along with the radio and dancing around the floor with the mop. When I commented that it was nice to see her feeling better, she thought I was making fun of her, so she picked up the teapot from off of the stove and fired it at me."

"Well...well...well..." I tooted.

Jobie continued to express his concern and frustration. Now, his biggest fear was that Sally and Betty Lou were experiencing symptoms similar to their mother's. "To make matters worse," he declared, "now that the girls are sent home from school, the place is beginning to talk."

Jobie's distress was justified. The mysterious disease afflicting the Rodgers' household had become the talk of the town. Rumours ran rampant. Many claimed that Dr. Templeman was dumbfounded as to the cause and, suspecting some sort of exotic, contagious virus, he was requesting the assistance of a specialist from the mainland. Aunt Daisy Snelgrove, Roaring Cove's hypochondriac, claimed that she had spoken to the Rodgers' children the same day they had been sent home from school and, within hours, was displaying similar symptoms herself. The telephone wires burned with talk about a curse that had been placed on the household because Jobie, a Protestant, had refused to become a Catholic, like Margaret, when they were married. Still others maintained that the water was the problem. It had been an extremely dry summer and most wells in the place were nearly dry, leaving the water stagnant and susceptible to contamination, and with Jobie's well lying just below the cemetery...

When Uncle Mark heard the rumours, he paid Jobie a visit to show his concern and to offer support. Uncle Mark, of course, was welcome at any house in Roaring Cove — especially Jobie's. For years Jobie has been competing with Winse Hillard for the title of best moonshine maker, and Uncle Mark made frequent visits to sample a new brew and to pass judgement. Consequently, Uncle Mark opened the back door and entered the porch, unannounced — the same as he had always done. As he did, he was met by Margaret.

"Come to sample the new batch have ya, Uncle Mark?" she asked.

"I had another purpose in mind for this visit, Margaret," Uncle Mark responded. "I came over to see you because I heard you weren't feeling well."

"Me? I'm as healthy as a horse and first rate — ready to dance and sing." Margaret snickered.

Then, without hesitation, she grabbed Uncle Mark by the arm and began dancing him around the porch floor. She hooted and hollered in a high-pitched voice that brought an embarrassed Jobie bursting through the kitchen door.

Jobie voiced his dissatisfaction in a stern but sympathetic tone, and Margaret immediately left the two men alone.

"You'll have to excuse Margaret," Jobie apologized, "She hasn't been herself lately."

Uncle Mark, well known for being forthright, gave his initial assessment of the situation, and he gave it to Jobie with both barrels.

"Jobie, she's drunk," Uncle Mark declared.

The blast of the comment nearly knocked Jobie off his feet. His eyes widened, his jaw drooped and his face drained of its colour. Several seconds lapsed before he could respond.

"Nonsense, Mark. You know as well as I do that Margaret never touched a drop of the stuff in her life."

"Well, I have never known her to," Uncle Mark agreed, "but you have to admit, she's acting mighty strange."

"She's foolish like that now, but give her an hour or so and she'll be lying down with a sick stomach and a headache," Jobie informed.

"You're sure she's not dipping into your moonshine when you're not looking?" Uncle Mark persisted.

"Well if she is," Jobie retorted, "the youngsters must be too because they're acting just as strange as their mother is."

Uncle Mark gently rubbed his chin with the palm of his hand and furrowed his forehead like he always does when he's pondering an issue. He quickly evaluated all the rumours he had heard. The only one that was plausible, as far as he was concerned, was the water theory. He questioned Jobie about it.

"What about the water, Jobie? Have you had it tested?"

"It's not the water," Jobie responded. "I've been boiling every drop since the weather turned hot. I even bought one of them new charcoal filtering jugs and I run the drinking water through it after I boil it. It takes away all that ground-like taste and it makes the water crystal clear."

"So them jugs really do work, do they?" Uncle Mark asked. "I'll have to get one, I s'pose. I heard that Sam Whiffen can't keep them in his shop."

"Work, indeed they do work. And, I'll share a secret with you about them, if you promise to keep it to yourself and not tell Winse Hillard."

"And what might that be?" Uncle Mark asked.

"They're the dandy rigs for taking the home-brew taste out of the moonshine," Jobie responded.

Uncle Mark sprang to attention like a man pricked with a pin. "What do you mean?" Uncle Mark asked anxiously.

"Well, if you let a brew sit for a few days, and then filter it through the jug, every bit of that home-brew aftertaste will be removed."

"How long have you been doing this?" Uncle Mark asked.

"Ever since I saw how well it worked to purify the water."

"Let me see that jug?" Uncle Mark requested.

Jobie disappeared into the kitchen and returned with the water jug. Uncle Mark promptly poured himself a drink of the crystalline substance. He swirled it in the glass and held it up to the light and gave it careful inspection. Like a connoisseur of fine wine, he sipped it through his front teeth and palatalized it for several seconds before swallowing.

After smacking his lips like a nursing baby, he asked, "has Margaret been drinking much of this water?"

"Yes, by the jugful. She's been continually thirsty since she's been sick," Jobie replied.

"And the girls too?"

"Equally so."

"Well," replied Uncle Mark, "'tis a wonder you're not put in jail, Jobie. This stuff is about 40 percent alcohol."

The mystery had been solved. Jobie had been straining his moonshine through the same jug from which his family had been drinking water. The strength of the liquor was being absorbed into the filter and becoming mixed with the drinking water. With each glass of water, Margaret and the girls were experiencing euphoria. After the ecstasy of this state subsided, they were subjected to the symptoms of withdrawal — better known as hangover. Each hangover brought a compelling thirst that was controlled by drinking more water, and the whole thing started over.

Within a day of Uncle Mark's discovery, Margaret, Betty-Lou and Sally were back to normal and a new rumour burnt the telephone wires of Roaring Cove. It seems that the women folk in Jobie's household had been bewitched by some strange and unknown entity and Jobie had summoned Uncle Mark White to charm away the curse. This he did by sprinkling purified water around the house and over the inflicted souls.

For Old Jack Only

"A puppy dog without a collar Annexed me on my evening walk; His coat suggested fleas and squalor, His tail had never known a dock. So humble, trusting, wistful was he, I gave his head a cautious pat, Then I regretted it because he accompanied me to my door-mat." Robert Service – Mongrel

No one knows exactly where Old Jack came from or how old he is. Some say he wandered into town from the neighbouring community of Kellop Harbour after being abandoned by a family that moved away to the mainland. Others claim that he was the mascot aboard a Portuguese ship and was accidentally left behind when the ship hastily left port after being investigated for selling contraband liquor to the locals. For years, this golden Labrador Retriever has been as much a part of Roaring Cove as is the government wharf. When he was younger, his days were spent following the children around, supervising their every activity. At mealtimes, any undesired leftovers were referred to as, "a bit for Old Jack," and were generously placed on peoples' front steps. At night, he crawled into the porch of any house with its back door left ajar. He is credited with saving two lives and Alf Lambert is credited with having saved his.

Lately though, Old Jack has fallen victim to his age. His brilliant golden coat has faded to a dusty colour, and arthritis has robbed him of his proud and spry prance. He still takes his occasional investigative stroll through town, but most of the time he spends curled up on the rug in front of my downstairs wood stove. You see, I have, more or less, adopted Old Jack in his old age – or maybe he has adopted me. In any case, I enjoy his company and he enjoys mine. When I take my doctor prescribed walks in around Roaring Cove Pond, Old Jack accompanies me, and we have an understanding that neither one of us will challenge the other. If I stop to rest or to talk with someone along the way, Old Jack waits patiently. When he stops to mark out his territory or to examine an unusual scent in the bushes, I wait for him.

I suppose it's because Old Jack and I spend so much time together that the newcomers living around Roaring Cove Pond assume that he belongs to me. That is why Mrs. Dorothy Taylor called me earlier in the summer and lambasted me because she had found Dilly, her pet poodle, lying dead in a pool of blood on her back bridge. The little dog had obviously been attacked and killed by some kind of vicious animal. Mrs. Taylor maintained that Old Jack was the only animal that roamed free in Roaring Cove; therefore, in her opinion, it was obviously he who had killed her precious Dilly.

Mrs. Taylor was one of the newcomers that had moved to Roaring Cove from outside the province when her husband filled a managerial position at the new fresh fish plant. She and the rest of her neighbours had been labelled, "higher-ups" because they separated themselves from the community and built fancy homes on the west side of Roaring Cove Pond. They rarely became involved in community activities, and they never learned to understand the ways of the Roaring Cove people. I knew of this woman's assertiveness because, several years earlier, I had been engaged in an altercation with her over accusations she had made against Silas Murphy, Roaring Cove's simpleton. At that time, I found myself compelled to come to Silas' defence. I now felt equally compelled to defend Old Jack.

"In all the years Old Jack has been in this community I, nor anyone else, have known him to hurt anyone or anything," I declared.

Not one to back away from an issue, Mrs. Dorothy Taylor continued with a litany of allegations about stray dogs and Old Jack in particular. I dismissed her claims as one would the odour from a toiling man on a hot day.

Nevertheless, her accusations had caused her neighbours to become suspicious about Old Jack, and I often noticed that a gate got closed inconspicuously or a pet was hastily beckoned inside when we were on our walks.

Even Nelson Hyde began doubting Old Jack. Nelson was the only one of the "higher-up" crowd with whom I had any kind of rapport. I had gotten to know him because he was a young man with three young children in school. Whenever I passed his house while on my walks, we'd engage in conversation and he'd pet Old Jack as we talked. Lately though, his gate has remained closed and our talks are conducted from over his fence while he pays absolutely no attention to Old Jack. The other day he got his message across by subtly pointing to a cage he had constructed for the family's pet rabbit.

"Look at the cage I constructed for Cuddles," he said pointing to a wire kennel attached to the side of the garage. "We used to let her run in the back yard, but Mrs. Taylor's poodle was killed by a wild animal earlier in the summer."

"I'm aware of that," I commented.

"The youngsters would be totally devastated if anything happened to their rabbit," he continued.

I wanted to remind Nelson that the last time Old Jack and I were inside his fence, Old Jack affectionately licked Cuddles until she looked like a wet mop. But I didn't. Old Jack and I continued our walk, undaunted.

I have always believed that a befriended dog is more reliable and loyal than most people are and Mrs. Dorothy Taylor and Nelson Hyde only confirmed my feeling. Last Saturday, though, something happened that caused me much dismay and to also doubt my theory.

It was a mauzie* morning with an eastern wind, thick fog and drizzly rain. A quick glance outside told me that my Saturday morning walk would be postponed, so I let Old Jack out to attend to his business. Usually, on mornings like this, he would be outside for only a few minutes and then come scratching at the door, requesting to be let in. This morning though he did not, and, when I opened the door to check on him, I noticed him meandering his way up Roaring Cove Pond Road.

"He's decided to go without me this morning," I thought. I had expected Old Jack to follow our usual route and to be gone at least an hour. Within fifteen or twenty minutes, though, I heard a familiar

---

*A damp, foggy day with drizzle.

scratching at the back door. I opened it. Old Jack ran into the front porch carrying something in his mouth. At first it looked like a muddy, soaked blanket. He ran past me, down the basement steps, and directly to his spot in front of the wood stove. It was there he dropped the thing that he was carrying. As I approached, I recognized the object as that of a limp and lifeless rabbit. At first, I assumed it was a wild rabbit that he had found in the woods or perhaps one that had been killed on the road. Nevertheless, when I examined it more closely, I saw that it was a white, domestic rabbit. It looked like Cuddles. My heart jumped into my throat.

"Jack, what in the world have you done?" I shouted in a reprimanding tone.

Without hesitation, I grabbed the dead rabbit, tucked it away in the wood box, donned my raincoat, and set out for Roaring Cove Pond Road. As I approached Nelson Hyde's place, I slowed down. Through the fog and rain I could barely make out the rabbit cage on the side of his garage. Sure enough, the door was ajar and the cage was empty. "Had Nelson let the rabbit out or had Old Jack managed to have opened the gate?" I wondered.

I did not want to believe my eyes. But the proof was home in my wood box. I turned and retraced my steps, my mind searching for a plan of action. By the time I reached home I had concocted a plan that would protect Old Jack.

I entered the house, took Old Jack by the scruff of the neck, led him out to the wood house and barred him in. "Now, my son," I said, "you're not to be seen for a few days."

Re-entering the house, I took the lifeless animal from the wood box, carried it into the bathroom and laid it in the sink. Using a soft face cloth, I washed the matted fur until it was free of mud. Next, I searched my wife's personal care basket and found a fancy bottle of "volumizing" shampoo for thin, fine hair. This I liberally poured over poor Cuddles and worked it into thick, foamy lather. After letting the shampoo stand for the amount of time indicated in the directions, I hung the rabbit on the showerhead by its back legs, turned on the hot water and gave it a thorough rinsing. Amazingly, the lustrous white colour returned to the furry coat. My next consideration was to get the fur dry. I was reaching for the big fleecy bath towel when I noticed the hair dryer hanging behind the door. "Perfect," I said aloud.

Like a professional hairdresser, I set the fan speed to the style position and I went to work. Using a quick jerking action to abruptly redirect the flow of the air, I blasted the fur so that it stood up and separated. In only a few minutes, Cuddles was once again a soft, velvety ball of fluff. I had worked miracles, but there was still one problem — the rabbit was dead.

The next part of my plan was executed with the skill of a thief in the night. I retrieved from the kitchen a plastic shopping bag, placed the dead rabbit in it, and again set off for Roaring Cove Pond Road. Under a protective blanket of thick fog, I jumped over Nelson Hyde's back fence, circled down around his garage and sneaked up to the empty rabbit's cage. I removed the limp bundle from the bag and gently placed it inside. Slowly, I closed the wire door, pocketed the empty bag and made a speedy exit for home.

"For Old Jack only," I muttered aloud as I kicked off my boots and settled in the old rocking chair in front of the wood stove. I felt a tinge of guilt for my actions, but at the same time, a sense of accomplishment for having denied Mrs. Dorothy Taylor the opportunity to take up another issue. After all, a dead rabbit in a kennel was no big deal — or was it?

Immediately after supper I looked outside and saw Uncle Mark White hobbling in through my gate. He had the flappers of his old bibbed cap hauled down around his ears and the tail of his overcoat was flying in the wind. He was in a hurry, and I knew he had news.

"The like was never known before," he breathlessly blurted out upon entering the kitchen.

"Why Uncle Mark, what has happened?"

"Something awful strange," he said. Then he stopped and waited to be encouraged to give more details.

"Strange? What do you mean, strange?" I asked.

"Yesterday morning Nelson Hyde went out to feed the pet

rabbit and found it dead in the cage."

"Yesterday morning? Are you sure it was yesterday?" I asked thinking that Uncle Mark had the time mixed up.

"Yes, yesterday," he answered. "Nelson told me himself. Why, did you hear the story already?"

"No...no..." I replied, realizing that Uncle Mark was very astute, and I had to be careful not to give anything away. "So, what's strange about finding a dead rabbit in a cage?" I asked.

"What's strange is that Nelson found the rabbit peacefully lying there like it had died in its sleep, so he took it and buried it in the woods on back of his shed."

"Buried it?" I asked. "That is strange."

"Yes, he buried it, but he left the door to the cage ajar and told the children the rabbit escaped into the woods. But, that's not the strange part. The strange part is, today, the children went out to the cage and found the rabbit lying there — dead — the same way Nelson had found it."

"Well that is strange indeed," I said, feeling relief for Old Jack and guilt for my actions.

"Indeed 'tis," said Uncle Mark. "Poor Nelson is half frightened to death; he thinks it's some kind of cruel joke because he lied to his children."

"Maybe, an animal dug it up," I added.

"Possible," replied Uncle Mark. "But how can you explain it ending up back in the cage?"

"I can't," I responded.

"I smell skullduggary,"* said Uncle Mark.

"Just wait until Mrs. Dorothy Taylor gets a hold of this." I remarked.

"I don't mind dat one," commented Uncle Mark. "She got a tongue on her like a Mountie's boot."

---

*To be up to some kind of badness or mischief.

Aunt Daisy's Letter

"The trouble with being a hypochondriac these days is that antibiotics have cured all the good diseases." – Caskie Stinnett

Uncle Mark White claims that Aunt Daisy Snelgrove is sick all of the time because she's a lonely woman who is seeking attention, and Dr. Templeman alleges she has, at one time or another, complained of every disease known to the medical world – and some that are yet to be invented. It is for this reason that Dr. Templeman frequently stamps "Hypochondria" across her chart and sends her off to the hospital in Middleville. In doing so, the good doctor alleviates himself of the aggravation of Aunt Daisy's constant whining. I, on the other hand, am inflicted with it because I have been driving Aunt Daisy to and from Middleville ever since I purchased my first car before the roads were paved. Consequently, on every trip to the hospital, I am forced to listen to a barrage of complaints.

Now, although nerve-racking and wearisome, these excursions are sometimes pleasantly amusing. You see, besides being known as a hypochondriac, Aunt Daisy is also perceived as a bit of an imbecile who often does things that are exceptionally humorous and enchanting. There was, for example, the time when she threw the entire hospital into pandemonium when she announced that she was haemorrhaging internally because she noticed she had passed blood while using the bathroom. She later realized that it was not blood at all – rather a result of having eaten several raw beets the previous night. On another occasion, after complaining of constipation, she went home and swallowed her entire prescription of suppositories. Yet another time, when she was unable to wear her dentures, she sucked the chocolate from an entire bag of chocolate-coated nuts and spit the remnants into a bowl. Jonas Pickett, as always, on the prowl for a handout, happened by and devoured the lot. These were the types of stories that I, as Aunt Daisy's private chauffeur, was privy to. The story I am about to relate came out during one of these drives.

Earlier this summer, Aunt Daisy called to inform me that her prostate was acting up and that she needed a ride to the hospital first thing in the morning. When I arrived to pick her up, Aunt Daisy was out on the road waiting for me.

"Where in the world were ya at? I thought you forgot about me." She complained as she climbed in the back seat.

It was like I had pressed the play button on a tape recorder; Aunt Daisy talked nonstop from Roaring Cove to Middleville. She started off by explaining to me that her inflamed prostate was cutting off her water. Of this she was certain because she had seen it on the *Medical Show* — her favourite television program.

"I loves to watch that show, you know, because I've had most of the stuff they talks about," she informed me.

She ended up by explaining to me how her "very close veins" had cut off the circulation in her feet causing her toenails to turn black. Only once did I interrupt to tell her that I didn't think she had a prostate.

"Stop talkin' and watch the road," she commanded.

Once in Middleville the routine was the same — a long wait at the hospital, and a longer one at the pharmacy. I stayed in the car and caught up on some reading.

Around noon I saw her coming across the parking lot, and I could see she was agitated. She was swinging her purse and strutting along like a military sergeant on a strategic war manoeuvre.

She jumped in the car and slammed the door. "There's some awful ignorant people in this world." she blurted.

"And why is that, Aunt Daisy?" I asked, knowing full well that I was about to get the full story.

"You wouldn't believe it," she said. " I had to wait for my prescription, so I sat on the bench in front of the lotto booth. I felt a small bit hungry, so I went over to the candy counter and bought myself a chocolate bar."

"What about your diabetes?" I asked.

"The doctor said my sugar was good. So, I decided I'd treat

myself — the first candy bar I had in months. Anyway, when I came back to my seat, this man was sitting in the very spot I had been sitting. I gave him a dirty look and sat on the other side of the bench."

"Well it is a public bench, Aunt Daisy. And there is room enough for more than one to sit."

"Yes, that's fair enough, but this fellar was a regular sleeveen."

"Why is that?" I asked.

"Why? He took the best part of me chocolate bar — that's why!" she snapped.

"Took your bar?"

"Yes, and he never had the courtesy to ask me. Now, if I thought the man was hungry, I would have bought him a bar. He didn't have to be deceitful about it."

"What do you mean, deceitful?"

"Well, I laid my bar on the bench between the two of us, and, before I knew it, this fellar reached over, opened it up, broke off a piece, and shoved it in his gob."*

"Did you say anything to him?"

"No! I was so stunned, I didn't know what to say, so I just broke off a piece for myself.

"I think I would have said something to him," I commented.

"I should have but I didn't — I just gave him another dirty look. And then, he had the gall to smile at me, and the brazen bugger took another piece."

"Another piece?" I asked

"Yes, another piece," Aunt Daisy answered. "But that's not all. That got me dander up, so I broke off two more pieces, and, when I did, he reached out and took all that was left. Then the bloody sleeveen got up and walked away without saying...thank you...kiss me arse...or anything."

For the rest of the way home, Aunt Daisy continued to express her outrage that anyone could be so despicable and ignorant as to take candy from a poor, sick woman. She sputtered and swore,

*Mouth.

squirmed in her seat and grew red in the face. By the time we reached her house, she had worked herself into a frenzy and claimed her blood pressure was on bust, and she was about to stroke out.

I figured that the candy bar episode would land Aunt Daisy in bed with one of her migraines and it would be a few days before I heard from her again. I was wrong. Early the next morning the telephone rang — it was Aunt Daisy and she sounded fine.

"If you're not busy, Schoolmaster, I wonder if you could drop over and help me write a letter to the newspaper?"

I promised her I would as soon as I finished a few chores. It was after lunch by the time I got to her house. She met me at the door.

"Where in the world were ya at?" she asked. "I thought you had forgotten about me. Now, sit down, I'll tell you what to say, and you write it down so 'tis suitable to be printed in the paper."

As opinionated as Aunt Daisy was, I had never known her to express her views in the public newspaper, so I was curious.

"What's all this about anyway Aunt Daisy?" I asked. "Why do you want to put a letter in the paper?"

"It's about what happened yesterday, with the candy bar up in Middleville," she announced.

"Don't you think you're taking this just a little too far, Aunt Daisy?" I queried. "I realize it wasn't very nice what that man did, but 'tis no need to make a big fuss over it."

"I'm not making a big fuss," she responded. "I want to write a letter of apology."

"A letter of apology? I don't understand."

"Well," says Aunt Daisy. "When I got home yesterday and opened me purse to get me pills, the first thing I saw was the candy bar I bought in the drug store."

"I thought the man ate most of your candy bar?"

"I thought so too," she responded. "But my bar is still in me purse so I must have eaten his."

"Aunt Daisy, that man must have thought you were some ignorant, or half starved to death," I teased.

"Now stop your tormentin' and take down the letter," she

commanded.

Aunt Daisy had obviously rehearsed the letter because she recited it from memory. I wrote it out word for word:

Dear Editor:

I thank you for space in your paper to write this letter of apology. On the afternoon of July 6, I entered the Middleville Mall and sat on a bench in front of the drug store. I would like to apologize to the gentleman who shared the bench with me because I accidentally took some of the chocolate bar he was eating. I was not feeling myself that day because, not being a well woman, I had just come from the hospital, and I mistook the bar the gentleman was eating for one that I bought only moments earlier. For that I am truly sorry, and I hope that the gentleman understands.

Sincerely,
Daisy M. Snelgrove (Roaring Cove)

Having business in Middleville the next day, I took Aunt Daisy's letter and dropped it off at the newspaper office. After I did, I strolled into the pharmacy to pick up a newspaper. The first thing I noticed on the candy counter was a large sign that read "All candy bars — two for the price of one."

"Well…well…well…" I mumbled aloud to myself. "Aunt Daisy was right all along."

My first impulse was to return to the newspaper office and withdraw the letter. It was obvious that the bar in Aunt Daisy's purse was the free one, and there was no need for her to apologize to anyone.

After careful consideration, I realized that Aunt Daisy was looking forward to seeing her letter in the paper, and I decided to keep everything to myself. This I did, until the paper came out and Uncle Mark read the letter. Immediately, he hurried to my house in pursuit of details.

"What's dis all about?" he asked, holding out the newspaper and pointing to Aunt Daisy's letter.

I told him everything.

Uncle Mark chuckled and said, "I tell you, dat woman would do anything for a bit of attention. When she goes to a funeral, she wants to be the corpse."

Shakespeare Would
Have Been Vexed

"All the world's a stage, And all the men and women merely players: They have their exits and their entrances; And one man in his time plays many parts..." William Shakespeare – *As You Like It*

For as long as I can remember the crowd from Roaring Cove has been holding a summer garden party to raise money for our volunteer fire department. It has always been a popular affair, attracting people all the way from Middleville to Kellop Harbour, and one year we even had in attendance a motorcycle gang from Texas. The event routinely takes place on the first weekend in July. Each year it starts off with a Friday morning pancake breakfast and ends up with a Sunday evening church service. In between, there are lobster boils and soup suppers, bingo games and card matches, dory races and horseback rides, square sets and sing songs, but the most popular event of all is inevitably an old-fashioned concert held in the schoolhouse. Since I have been the Schoolmaster in Roaring Cove, I have had the privilege of organizing this event. It has always been one from which I have taken great pleasure. This year though the concert was different.

It was Thumb-On-Wrench Swyers, Roaring Cove's Mayor, who came up with the idea of turning our garden party into a week long "come home year" celebration. Invitations were sent to flamboyant politicians and loquacious media personnel. Anyone who had lived in or moved away from Roaring Cove was sent a special letter of invitation. Advertisements were taken out in all the local papers and a huge sign on the highway directed tourists to our festivities.

The planning for the event began prior to Christmas. Committees were formed to look after everything from music to toilet facilities, and I was told by Thumb-On, in no uncertain terms, that this year's concert had to be the best ever. This made me quite anxious about my responsibility, so I wasted no time calling a meeting. The same old crowd, the ones I refer to as the Roaring Cove Players, showed up and all had ideas for a brilliant show. As usual, all the women wanted the men to dress in women's clothing and hold a beauty pageant. Thankfully, Harold Buffett, the queen of last year's pageant, vehemently opposed this suggestion because, while being crowned, he had fallen off his high-heels and torn a ligament in his leg.

"I can do a recitation, the same as I did last year," volunteered Toby Avery.

"And I'll sing Newfie Outhouse again," said Marie House.

"Seeing 'tis going to be a special time,* I think we should make up one this year," commented Hayward Green.

"I was thinking the same thing, Hayward," I said. "What did you have in mind?"

"Well," responded Hayward, "I think it would be a good laugh to make up one about the time Aunt Daisy lost her false teeth overboard, or about the time Jonas Pickett got stuck in his outhouse."

Aunt Daisy came to her taps and voiced her objection, "dat's just what you would come up with, Hayward, something to push a bit of fun at someone else."

I was rather inclined to agree with Aunt Daisy. Thumb-On's comments had been playing heavy on my mind, and I had reached the conclusion that it was time for us to stop making fun of ourselves and putting ourselves down. It was time for the crowd from Roaring Cove to show that we could put on a sophisticated show as well as anyone else.

"I think we should do something by Shakespeare," I announced

"By who?" echoed the entire crowd.

"By William Shakespeare, the greatest playwright who ever lived."

My suggestion was received like a fart in church. I was accused of being highfalutin and told that I was off my head.

---

*A party or celebration.

"What do the likes of Roaring Covers know about actin' that kind of stuff?" asked Hayward Green.

"I think we should do an old-fashioned concert the way we always did," said Sam Whiffen, and everyone agreed with him.

My reputation was on the line so I was not about to back down. "The Mayor wants something special because its "come home year," so I think I should get to choose," I declared.

The meeting became noisy and rambunctious, and it continued until midnight. We emerged with a compromise. Toby was to deliver a recitation, Marie was to sing Newfie Outhouse, and there was to be a variety of other songs. The male beauty contest was to be saved for the Christmas concert; and, reluctantly, they agreed to attempt any two Shakespearean scenes – of my choosing.

By the time we met for our first rehearsal, I had decided upon the Witches' scene from Macbeth and the balcony scene from Romeo and Juliet. I presented my selections cautiously to the crowd, and, much to my surprise, they gave their overwhelming approval. When I asked for volunteers to play the Shakespearean parts, I was stunned when all enthusiastically offered themselves. I should have twigged something at that time, but I didn't. And, for the first time in the history of the Roaring Cove concerts I was compelled to hold auditions.

"Sure 'tis just like Hollywood," voiced Aunt Daisy as she was trying out for one of the witches. And, grotesquely thrown out of shape because of age and arthritis, she was quite convincing in the role and landed it without question.

The other two weird, bearded creatures from the underworld were equally easy to cast. Penelope Whiffen, who was referred to by the children as Witch Whiffen, because of her bony frame, dagger sharp facial features, and wispy grey-black hair, was an easy pick.

Harold Buffett landed the part of the third witch because he greatly resembled a testosterone producing female with a maldow* looking beard he had nurtured to compensate for the fact that he went bald when he was twelve.

---

*A mossy hair-like substance that hangs on spruce and fir trees.

Winse and Elsie Hillard had only just celebrated twenty-five years of nuptial bliss and had been going around town like two young pups in heat. Consequently, they brought their renewed passions to the parts of Romeo and Juliet.

Once the parts were selected, though, and we began rehearsing in earnest, the Shakespearean thespians became lackadaisical and inattentive. It took them forever to learn their lines, they giggled through each practice, and they constantly showed up twenty minutes late. When I questioned them about their tardiness, the explanation was always the same.

"We had a previous meeting."

Again I should have twigged something, but I didn't. The closer we got to the production date the more disheartened I became, and the more I equated my cast with the crude mechanicals who performed the Pyramus and Thisbe play. When Thumb-On called to advise me that, because of popular demand, it was necessary to add a matinee, I felt as if I really was in a midsummer night's dream.

By the time the day of the concert arrived, Roaring Cove somewhat resembled a refugee camp. Most cars had different coloured license plates, there were tents and campers everywhere and every mother's son and daughter had come home. As I made my way to the school for the first show, the term "my nerves are rubbed raw" had taken unprecedented meaning. My legs felt as if they were slowly melting and a thousand electrical impulses were firing repeatedly in my stomach.

When the curtain opened for the matinee, Reverend King, who was the emcee for the event, welcomed everyone and told the joke he always told about the Bishop meeting St. Peter. When the time came for the Shakespearean scenes, he assumed his ringmaster's tone and flamboyantly made the announcement.

"Now ladies and gentlemen, we have a special treat for you. For the first time ever, the Roaring Cove Players have prepared for you two scenes by the master playwright of all time, William Shakespeare."

Suddenly, there was a drum roll and the stage lights came up on

Aunt Daisy, Penelope and Harold. All were dressed in black, tattered clothing, and were circling a big bark pot* we had borrowed from Albert Hicks. Aunt Daisy, the first witch, started off, and much to my surprise, all three went through the scene and did not forget a line.

Aunt Daisy: *Trice the brinded cat hath mewed.*
Penelope: *Trice and once the hedge—pig whined.*
Harold: *Harpier cries; 'tis time; 'tis time*
Aunt Daisy: *Round about the cauldron go;*
In the poison entrails throw.
Toad, that under cold stone
Days and nights has thirty-one
Sweltered venom sleeping got,
Boil thou first I' the charmed pot.
All: *Double, double toil and trouble:*
Fire burn, and cauldron bubble.
Harold: *Scale of dragon, tooth of wolf,*
Witches mummy, maw and gulf
Of the ravin'd salt-sea shark,
Root of hemlock digg'g I' the dark,
Liver of blaspheming Jew,
Gall of goat, and slips of yew
Slivered in the moon's eclipse
Nose of Turk and Tartar's lips,
Finger of birth-strangled babe
Ditch delivered by a drab.
Make the gruel thick and slab.
Add thereto a tiger's cauldron,
For the ingredients of our cauldron.
All: *Double, double toil and trouble:*
Fire burn, and cauldron bubble.
Penelope: *Cool it with a baboon's blood,*
Then the charm is firm and good

---

*Bark is a substance used to preserve nets and line. The bark pot is a iron pot in which the bark is boiled.

Harold:	*A drum, a drum! Macbeth doth come.*
All:	*The weird sisters, hand in hand,*
	Posters of the sea and land,
	Thus do go about, about,
	Trice to thine, and trice to mine,
	And trice again to make up nine.
Aunt Daisy:	*When shall we three meet again?*
	In Thunder, lighting or in rain?
Penelope:	*When the Hurly Burly's done,*
	When the battle is lost and won!
Harold:	*That will be ere the set of sun.*
Aunt Daisy:	*Where the place?*
Penelope:	*Upon the heath.*
Harold:	*There to meet with Macbeth.*
All:	*Fair is foul, and foul is fair,*
	Hover through the fog and filthy air.

The three pretended to be flying and soured offstage. The curtain fell and there was polite applause from the audience. Once backstage, there was relief and there was jubilation. Aunt Daisy, Harold and Penelope hugged and congratulated each other on a job, they thought, well done. I was happy with the performance and I began to relax a little. I complimented the players, but I was quick to warn them not to get too giddy because they had a later performance.

"Oh don't you worry, Schoolmaster," confirmed Harold, "the next show will be the heck of a lot better than that one."

"That's good, keep up the confidence," I responded and I was off to help prepare the stage for the Romeo and Juliet scene. Reverend King entertained the audience with another joke while Uncle Mark and I rolled the balcony, the one he had built, to the stage. Elsie, looking elegant in her Juliet costume, climbed onto the balcony, leaned her elbow on the railing and prepared herself for the scene. Winse tugged at the crotch of his purple tights and positioned himself on one knee in a dramatic pose. I poked Reverend King through the curtain to indicate we were ready.

"And now ladies and gentlemen, the Roaring Cove Players have prepared but another Shakespearean scene for you. So, sit back and enjoy this beautiful love scene from Romeo and Juliet!"

As soon as the curtain was drawn, Alfie Lambert, in an attempt to befuddle Winse, shouted from the audience, "nice legs Winse." The remark threw a few giggles from the viewers, but Winse was as solid as a grump* set in cement and commenced, undaunted.

Winse:	*"But, soft! What light through yonder window break?*
	It is my lady, o, it is my love!
	See how she leans her cheek upon
	Her hand! O that I were a glove
	Upon that hand, that I might touch that cheek.
Elsie:	*Ay me!*
Winse:	*She speaks! O speak again, bright angel!*
	For thou art as glorious to this night,
	Being o'er my head, as a winged messenger of heaven.
Elsie:	*O Romeo, Romeo! Wherefore art thou Romeo?*
	Deny thy father and refuse thy name.
	Or if thou wilt not be but sworn my love,
	And I'll no longer be a Capulet.
Winse:	*I take thee at thy word. Call me*
	But love, and I'll be new baptized;
	Henceforth, I never will be Romeo.
Elsie:	*What man art thou that thus bescreen'd in night*
	So stumblest on my counsel.
Winse:	*My name, dear saint, is hateful to myself,*
	Because it is an enemy to thee.

*A wooden post on a wharf to which boats are tied.

Elsie:	*Art thou not Romeo and a Montague:*
	If they see they, they will murder thee.
Winse:	*Alack, there lies more peril in thine eye*
	Than twenty of their sword!
Elsie:	*By whose direction found'st thou out this*
	place?
Winse:	*By love, that first did prompt me to inquire.*
Elsie:	*Dost thou love me? O gentle Romeo.*
	If thou dost love me, pronounce it faithfully.
Winse:	*Lady, by yonder blessed moon I swear*
	That tips with silver all these — tree tops.
Elsie:	*Although I joy in thee, I have no*
	joy in this contact tonight.
	It is too rash, too unadvised, too sudden
	Sweet, good night, good night!
Winse:	*O, wilt thou leave me so unsatisfied?*
Elsie:	*What satisfaction canst thou have tonight?*
Winse:	*The exchange of though faithful vow for mine.*
Elsie:	*Three words, dear Romeo, and good night*
	indeed.
	If thy bent of love be honourable,
	Thy purpose marriage, send word tomorrow.
Winse:	*So thrive my soul—*
Elsie:	*A thousand times good night!*
	Good night, good night! Parting is such
	sweet sorrow."

The applause started before the curtain closed, and it was thunderous and sustained. Winse and Elsie had played the part with conviction and sincerity, and they proved to all that Roaring Covers could indeed do sophisticated theatre. A huge weight had been lifted from my shoulders, and I relaxed for the first time in months.

Thumb-On-Wrench was the first one backstage to offer his congratulations. "A very fine show indeed!" he proclaimed.

Soon others came around to give their nod of approval. The

players soaked up the praise and wore their new celebrity status like children with new shoes. I again reminded everyone to stay focused for the second show, and as I was doing so, the players did an unusual thing. They bunched around me and insisted that I was to watch the second show with the audience.

"You've worked hard enough," commented Penelope. "We can get everything ready."

"That's right, you've prepared a good show, so you should get the chance to enjoy it, same as everyone else," added Aunt Daisy.

"But you'll need me back here," I protested.

"Nonsense, we have already proven we can do a good show."

I continued to object, but it fell on deaf ears. And, as soon as the doors opened for the upcoming show, the entire cast of the Roaring Cove Players, along with Reverend King, ushered me to a reserved seat in the front row. I should have twigged something, but I was flattered with the group's thoughtfulness.

Before Reverend King introduced the first act, he acknowledged me and invited me to stand to be recognized. I felt the tips of my ears burning as the audience applauded.

Toby Avery started off with his recitation. It was well received, as were the other acts. But I was most anxious to observe the response to the Shakespearean finale. Judging from the earlier group, I was certain that it would be appreciated. Anxiety quickly transformed to horror when the curtain opened. There was no bark pot. Rather, it had been replaced by a slop pail.* The witches no longer looked like witches. Harold was dressed in a suit of oilskins with rubber boots and cape ann.* Aunt Daisy had on a pair of home made logans,* a bright pink, flaring skirt, red plaid jacket, and a bandanna tied tightly around her head. Penelope was decked in a set of one-piece, fleece-lined long johns with the trap door conspicuously open. The smell told everyone in the first ten rows that the players had been to the fish plant and collected fish offal. They circled the slop

---

*A vessel kept in the bedroom used as a portable toilet.
*An oilskin cap worn by fisherman.
*A popular work boot with a rubber bottom and a leather leg that extends almost to the knee.

pail and began dropping this awful substance into it.

I was stupefied as to what to do. My immediate impulse was to jump up and stop this mockery, but the audience was applauding, so I slumped in my seat suddenly twigging what I should have twigged months ago. The performers continued...

Aunt Daisy:	*Twice from across the bay the bitch in heat whined.*
Penelope:	*Twice from the harbour ice Old Jack whined back.*
Harold:	*Open water in between, so he chose to sit and whine: until to the ice his scrotum it froze.*
Aunt Daisy:	*Round about the slop pail go, In the rotten cod guts throw. Lump fish stuck to an old rock. Hot vomit strained through a dirty sock.*
All;	*Double, double over with cramp. Fetch the pail and light the lamp.*
Penelope:	*Shell of wrinkle,* mussel, clam and snail Put to boil and stew in our pail. Eye of conner* on a hook Hung to steam, char and cook. Spawn of caplin* and ink of squid, Scale of salmon, jigger of lead, For a charm to put away a wart. In a little cod liver oil squirt.*
All:	*Double, double over with cramp, Fetch the pail and light the lamp.*
Harold:	*Claw of crab and fin of flounder,*

---

*Salt water snail.
*An ocean perch found around fishing wharves. Catching conners was a popular sport for the children.
*A small smelt-like fish; the preferred source of food for cod.

> Maggots from a soggy rounder.*
> Dog fish teeth and sculpin's* lips
> Barnacles of a sunken ship.
> Bilge water* from a leaky punt.
> Blood of those who protest the hunt.
> Blubber drained from a puncheon tub,
> On the rim of our pail we'll rub.
> Pus from a water pup,*
> Scullin' oar* to mix it up.
> Make our charm to cure all hurts,
> Especially frostbite, cramps and warts.

Penelope: *A gun! A gun!*
> *Look, Schoolmaster, what we have done!*

All: *The Roaring Cove Players, hand in hand,*
> *Simple folk of the sea and land.*
> *Thus, around the slop pail go*
> *In such a way to let you know,*
> *Whether concert or Shakespearean play,*
> *We are proud players from the bay.*

Aunt Daisy: *What play shall we do next?*
Penelope: *One to make Shakespeare vexed?*
Harold: *Or one to make the Schoolmaster glad?*
Aunt Daisy: *One to make Winse and Elsie sad.*
Harold: *Look out, we come, my son!*
> *'Cause our play is nearly done.*

All: *Fair is foul, and foul is the air,*
> *'Cause our secret with you we did share.*

The sound of an accordion music filled the hall, and the three devious characters broke into a lively tap dance, and danced their

---

*A young cod fish.
*A thorny, scavenger fish with a large head and mouth.
*Water that accumulates in the bottom of a boat.
*A blister or sore that forms on the skin of fishermen.
*A oar that is used to propel a small boat by inserting it through a hole in the stern and twisting it in a particular way.

way offstage. The lights went black, the curtain fell, the audience sprang to its feet in applause, and I headed for the door. I was not to get very far, though. I was swamped by the familiar and unfamiliar alike. They patted me on the back and shook my hand.

"Well done, Schoolmaster!"

"We knew you'd put a twist to it."

"Very entertaining."

"Good job, old chap!"

My look of bewilderment was interrupted as bashfulness, and, before I knew it, I was sitting back down in my seat and Reverend King was introducing the Romeo and Juliet scene. As soon as the curtain opened, I knew I was again to be the victim of bold duplicity. Elsie was sitting in a rocking chair. A kerosene lamp was burning next to her and she was furiously working a set of knitting needles. She was dressed in a long flannelette nightgown with a pair of homespun vamps* on her feet. Her hair was tightly wound up in rollers. The audience immediately began to laugh. As the laughter was subsiding, Winse poked his head through the backstage entrance and peeped out at Elsie.

He addressed the audience, "Good Lord, someone got a lamp left burning. Oh, 'tis Elsie. Sure I'm gone on she. Oh see how her fingers work them needles. Oh I wish I was a vamp on dem needles dat I might touch dem beautiful, nimble fingers."

Oblivious to Winse and the audience, Elsie raised her leg and broke wind. Winse, in rubbers boots, coveralls and a salt and pepper cap, jumped onto the stage...

Winse:	*Ay, she got gas, dat's why she's up. Oh! fart again my precious trout 'cause seeing you tonight is worth a thousand farms down south.*
Elsie:	*Oh, Winse, Winse, where in the world is ya at? Oh, Winse, why are you a Protestant from Roaring Cove instead of a*

*Woollen stockings.

41

	Catholic from Kellop Harbour?
Winse:	Say you'll have me and I'll turn. I'll turn to a Catholic quicker than you can cast off dat vamp.
Elsie:	Whose dat at dis hour? You dat peepin' tom dat's been goin' round glowering in people's windows? Make one step farther towards me and I'll stab ya with me needles.
Winse:	Hold ya tongue, Elsie. The next thing you'll have ya old man up. 'Tis me — Winse.
Elsie:	Winse? You gone off ya head or what? What in the name of God is ya doin' over here at this hour? If the old man catches ya, he'll rip ya open from nave to chops!
Winse:	So be it. I'd rather be split like a cod than go another day without seeing ya.
Elsie:	How did you get to Kellop Harbour tonight?
Winse:	I came across on harbour ice.
Elsie:	You foolish thing. 'Tis hardly caught over, you could have fell through and drowned.
Winse:	Elsie, I'd swim across if 'twas no other way.
Elsie:	Oh, my poor foolish love struck Winse, do you think dat much about me?
Winse:	Yes Elsie, you knows I do…and besides…I got something I wants to ask ya.
Elsie:	You do?
Winse:	Yes Elsie, I wants…I wants…you know…I wants…
Elsie:	Come on, my son, out with it.
Winse:	Elsie, I wants…I wants me and you…to tie the knot.
Elsie:	Oh, I'd love to Winse, but you knows as well as I do, the old man would go right straight off his head. He'd never consent for me to marry anyone other than a Catholic.

Winse:	*Then I'll turn…I'll be as good a Catholic as…the Pope.*
Elsie:	*The only Catholic is a born Catholic as far as the old man is concerned.*
Winse:	*Ay, the devil with the old man. Let me take you up to Middleville; we can get hitched up there.*
Elsie:	*When?*
Winse:	*In the spring, when the ice breaks up. I'll come over in the punt and you meet me down on Manuel's Point.*
Elsie:	*Oh Winse! I know ya heart is in the right spot, but you caught me off guard. I got to t'ink about it.*
Winse:	*But I can't stand not knowin'.*
Elsie:	*Tomorrow…I'll send word tomorrow…and now my poor foolish Winse, good night, good night. And, do be careful on that harbour ice.*

The lights slowly faded out and Winse and Elsie turned to the audience and took a slow bow. They were quickly joined by the other players and all performed the curtain call that we had rehearsed. The place went up! Everyone jumped to their feet and whistled and cheered. It was obvious that the show had been thoroughly enjoyed. I tried to make for the door, but Reverend King called me to the stage. I made a courteous appearance and was again recognized by the audience.

"So, Schoolmaster, what did you think of that?" Harold asked grinning from ear to ear.

"I think Shakespeare would have been vexed," I responded.

A Good Piece of Play

(The Hockey Game That Lasted Eight Months)

"A healthy nation is as unconscious of its nationality as a healthy man of his bones. " George Bernard Shaw — *John Bull's Other Island*

Hockey came to Roaring Cove with the coming of Confederation in 1949, and Uncle Mark, a self-proclaimed anti-confederate, claims that it was the only positive thing Roaring Cove acquired from the coalition.

Soon after all the papers were signed and it became official — we were Canadians — the radio stations began broadcasting the games, and Uncle Mark kept the batteries fully charged and the dial button finely tuned.

When the power line followed the road into Roaring Cove in the 1960s and we acquired electricity, Uncle Mark purchased the first television set in the place, for no other reason than to watch hockey. Each Saturday night every man, whose wife would allow, crowded into Uncle Mark's house to root for his favourite team. It was the social event of the week with lots of cheering and a good many arguments.

The next winter the Eagles, Roaring Cove's first hockey team was formed, and Uncle Mark became its biggest fan. He never missed a game, be it a serious contest with another place or a fun skirmish among the local boys.

Over time, however, the hockey excitement had died away. The Eagles have long since folded and there hasn't been a good sheet of ice on the pond in years.

Earlier this winter, though, some of that old excitement reappeared because of the Olympic Games. Canada's team had been playing very well and Uncle Mark was as excited as a mainlander over it. As a matter of fact, he invited a bunch of us to his house to watch the gold medal game.

"It'll be just like old times!" he proclaimed.

Six or seven of us accepted the invitation and arrived at Uncle Mark's shortly after supper. As we entered his gate, Gideon Forward pointed to the flagpole. "I never thought I'd see it," he said. The Maple Leaf was flying next to the Union Jack.

The national anthem was being played when we clustered around Uncle Mark's television set. From the time the opening puck was dropped to the end of the first period, we barely spoke a word. During the first intermission, though, we began reminiscing about old times and the games on the pond. We agreed that the most memorable game of all was the one that took eight months to complete, and, among us all we pieced together every detail of that legendary game as if it had happened yesterday.

The Eagles had been waiting all winter for a rematch with Kellop Harbour. The Kellop Harbour Sea Dogs had walloped the Eagles a stunning twenty-six to one the previous year in a game held on the harbour ice up in Kellop Harbour, and the Eagles were anxious to settle the score at home. Each week the snow was shovelled off Roaring Cove Pond, and the ice was flooded in preparation for the big challenge. However, that winter was one of many storms, and, as fast as an icy spot was cleared off, it quickly drifted in. It was not until St. Patrick's Day that Mother Nature gave her permission for the match to go ahead. There had been a mild spurt and it had rained for three consecutive days. Then the mercury dropped just enough to transform Roaring Cove Pond into a natural sheet of quicksilver.

The game was scheduled to start at ten o'clock, and, just after daybreak, Tacker Manuel was on the pond inspecting the ice. As soon as a few young fellows gathered around, he summoned their help to drag Toby Avery's rodney onto the pond and turn it bottom up. Then he perched himself atop of it to officiate the game. As soon as the Eagles showed up, the rest of Roaring Cove began to meander towards the pond. When ten o'clock came and there was still no sign of the Kellop Harbour players, the spectators became fearful that the game was off. Rumours quickly spread that the Sea

Dogs were afraid to play us on home ice. Another theory was that the entire Kellop Harbour team had gone on a bender and was too drunk to care about hockey. By and by though, about half past ten, Tacker spotted the invading troops.

"Here they come!" Tacker shouted from his perch atop of the rodney.

All eyes turned to see the Kellop Harbour Sea Dogs silhouetted against the morning sky as they marched in a single file over the Roaring Cove Hills. With gunnysacks strapped to their back, and skates swinging from the end of their hockey sticks, they indeed looked like a threatening force.

"We thought you had gone astray," Tacker bellowed when they came within an earshot.

"All of the brooks is out because of the run off from the rain," answered the big fellow with a bushy red beard. "There was several times we thought we'd have to turn back."

"Well, we'd better hurry up and get started," retorted Tacker. "'Tis going to be a mild day and the ice will be gettin' soft."

Several of the Kellop Harbour players voiced an objection. "We're too tired to play right away; we've been walkin' since daylight."

"You'll not get the upper hand by playin' an exhausted team," one of them remarked.

"Ya, we gotta take a spill,"*

No one could dispute the logic of the argument and Kellop Harbour was given a half-hour rest period. It was after eleven before the Sea Dogs laced up their skates; then they wanted to discuss the rules. Both teams flocked around Tacker. Would there be risers or no risers? The Eagles maintained that rising the puck could result in someone getting injured. The Sea Dogs pointed out that high shots were a part of the game and should be permitted. The Eagles countered by pointing out that the Sea Dogs had catalogues laced to their shins and a flying puck was less of a threat to them. Tacker, trying to be fair-minded, ruled that the Eagles could have also used catalogues if they had foresight enough. Therefore, for the first time

---

*A rest.

in Roaring Cove, riser shots were to be permitted.

Next, the Sea Dogs protested the use of boots as goal post. Boots could be easily moved and were not reliable enough to mark out the goal area. They claimed that heavy rocks would be better substitutes. Rocks could not be easily shifted and if struck with the puck could give a rebound and a consequent scoring opportunity. Tacker was in agreement and four huge beach stones were retrieved from the barachois. The Sea Dogs also insisted that boots were not to be worn by any player — hockey was a skating game and it should be played like it is up in Canada. Tacker knew that the Eagles' goalie, Chubby Charlie Freak, could not wear skates because he was born with a club foot, and Art Pearce, their best player, did not own a pair. Thus, he ruled that boots would be tolerated — after all it was to the Sea Dogs' advantage because players wearing boots were hindered in their movement on ice.

The game was to be ninety minutes long. The only time-outs were to be for injuries and undetermined reasons.

It was well after eleven before all the rules were determined, and Tacker instructed both teams to start the game. The Sea Dogs skated to the far end of the pond and disappeared behind the small point of land that juts out from the south side shore.

"Where are they all gone now?" Jonas Pickett shouted. "They all get short taken or what?"

Shortly, though, the Sea Dogs emerged in grand fashion and skated up the ice. They were led by the goalie who was wearing a huge set of homemade goalie pads and carrying a hand-crafted goalie stick. His pads were simple burlap bags stuffed with some substance that had the consistency of sawdust, and his stick was an ordinary one with a piece of one-by-six spruce fastened to its shaft. All of the Sea Dogs had now removed their parkas and underneath they were wearing sweaters of various shades of green. Each player was wearing a number made from white sticking plaster. The like had never been seen in Roaring Cove. We were uncertain whether the display was an attempt to intimidate the Eagles or if it was in honour of St. Patrick's Day.

Now it was the Eagles turn to protest. If Kellop Harbour wanted to wear green, it was up to them, and the use of catalogues as shin pads was bad enough, but the goalie pads and stick were stacking the deck too far in the visiting team's favour.

Once again Tacker was called on to make a ruling. After careful deliberation he determined that goalie pads and goalie sticks were standard equipment up in Canada, so it should be permitted in Roaring Cove. To be fair, and considering the fact that the Sea Dogs were given time to take a spill, the Eagles were given equal time to secure goalie equipment.

Without hesitation, Alfie Lambert and Joe Stead set out in two different directions. Alfie crossed the pond, climbed the bank into Toby Avery's garden, entered his root cellar, dumped two sacks of potatoes into the bin and returned with the two empty sacks. Joe scampered across the road, onto Mrs. Dorothy Taylor's lawn, ripped a picket from the fence that surrounded her rose bushes, and returned with it — nails intact. Quickly, seaweed was gathered from Roaring Cove Beach and stuffed into the bags. The painter* was cut from Toby's rodney and used to lace the bags to Chubby Charlie's legs and a rock was used to hammer the picket to his stick.

It was noon before the puck was dropped. Straightaway, Alfie Lambert flicked the puck over to Joe Stead. Quick as the lamp lighter, Joe dodged around three of the Sea Dogs and fired the puck up to Art Pearce who was in the clear.

"A good piece of play!" shouted Uncle Mark.

But, with the ice as slippery as it was, Art's boots had little grip and he was easily overtaken by the agile number seven from Kellop Harbour. Number seven flicked a pass back to big number four, the fellow with the bushy red beard. This brute of a chap cocked his wrist and let fire at Chubby with a vicious riser. Chubby saw the projectile coming and fearing the consequence of the impact, ducked out of the way.

One to nothing for Kellop Harbour.

The play continued and within a few minutes, number four

---

*A rope used to fasten a boat to a wharf.

again had the puck and let drift with a blistering blast. This time, Chubby was uncertain of which way to move to avoid the blow; he froze between the two goal posts. It struck him square between the legs, and Chubby went down with pain. Notwithstanding the fact that most of the women in Roaring Cove were present, Chubby Charlie held his private parts and rolled around the ice for the best part of fifteen minutes. This was considered time out and the puck had to be dropped again. Within minutes the bearded number four again miraculously had control. He turned and took aim at Chubby. Chubby took flight leaving the goal wide open.

Two to nothing for Kellop Harbour.

By now, the sun was high in the sky and the ice was beginning to soften. Consequently, Art Pearce's boots began to stick to the ice and he got footing. He worked his way toward the Sea Dogs' end and got off a riser shot. The puck ricocheted off the goalie's big pad and went behind him.

"A good piece of play!" hollered Uncle Mark and all hands began to cheer.

"Over the post," disputed the Sea Dogs and immediately a fuss broke out.

The Eagles were adamant it was a goal and the Sea Dogs insisted that it wasn't. The argument was heated and sustained. By and by the big number four made the mistake of pushing Sylvester Hicks. Now everyone in Roaring Cove knows that Sylvester has the fuse of a powder keg — as did his father and grandfather before him. Number four obviously didn't, and before he knew what was happening, Sylvester was in his face with both fists flying. Instantly, all hands were in it, and the biggest racket ever seen in Roaring Cove developed. Even Aunt Daisy Snelgrove joined in and smacked one of the Kellop Harbour players over the head with her purse, and Walt Churchill and I had to hold back Uncle Mark. When things got seriously ugly, Toby Avery broke it up.

A shotgun blast ripped over the ice. All hands froze and looked for the source of the explosion. Toby was standing atop of his rodney with his double-barrel breech loader* high in the air.

"You fellars want to fight or play hockey?" he asked.

The question was a rhetorical one and the players separated. Tacker took advantage of the moment and declared Art's shot a goal.

Two to one — Kellop Harbour.

There was some sulking among the Sea Dogs, and a further delay because all of their numbers had become unstuck during the ruckus and were strewn over the playing area. By the time the numbers were sorted out and reattached, the warm sun had turned the ice to slush. Everyone agreed that playing on the soft ice would only tear it up, and the logical thing to do was to wait until later in the afternoon when the day cooled off and the ice firmed up.

Most of the spectators went home, the Eagles jammed into Toby's twine loft, and the Sea Dogs retreated into the woods on the south side of the pond, made a fire and had a mug up.*

Around three o'clock the wind chopped to the northwest and the temperature went down like a sinking ship. In a matter of minutes, the ice had hardened so Tacker summoned the players and dropped the puck. The play continued for only a few minutes when the big number four rifled a shot at Chubby. Lucky for Chubby the bearded monstrosity missed his mark and the puck travelled the full width of the pond and went smack into Aunty Daisy's slop pail pile. In the winter, all the people in Roaring Cove dumped their slop pails on the frozen beach in front of their houses. When the ice melted in the spring, the tide flushed the accumulated pile out to sea. Aunt Daisy's slop pail pile had grown considerably over the winter and was an easy target.

Players from each team chased the puck and began digging for it. Because of the mildness of the day, the pile had thawed allowing the puck to become embedded somewhere near its core. The frantic players battled for possession, until the sleeping stench was disturbed. Simultaneously, the disillusioned players pinched their noses and retreated. A lost puck — a time out was called.

*A common name for a shot gun.
*A small lunch had in the woods by boiling the tea kettle over an open fire.

The search went out for another puck. For a while it seemed as if there was not one in the whole of Roaring Cove. Then, Albert Hicks remembered that he had found a black rubber thing in the bottom of the barrel of clothes he had come from the States and didn't know what it was. He went home to search for it. Twenty-five minutes later he was back. Paddy Whalen recognized it as a doughnut gasket off a tractor. It wasn't a hockey puck, but it would have to do.

It was a little after four o'clock when Tacker dropped the gasket. No sooner had he done so when Bobby Johnson drew back with a golf shot and sent the phoney puck rolling the length of the pond. Unbeknownst to anyone, Old Jack had made his way onto the ice during the time out. He spotted the rolling object, and his natural instinct emerged — retrieve. With deadly precision he snatched the rolling disc in his mouth and began to return with it. Suddenly, he noticed four players charging down on him with sticks swinging; he became spooked and bolted in over the Roaring Cove Barrens. Margaret Rodgers found the thing two years later while blueberry picking. Another time out was called and a search was organized for another puck — or a reasonable facsimile.

After searching for approximately half an hour, the best that anyone could find was a solid rubber ball. It was getting late so it would have to do - there had been many hockey games in the past played with a ball.

The sun was hanging low in the sky when the ball was dropped. The Sea Dogs were determined to take control of the match. Immediately, number six, one of the smallest, nimblest players set up big number four so that he was face to face with Chubby. He drove the ball at the goal with such force the softer rubber material was catapulted out of shape and it emitted a sound similar to that of a boiling kettle. But Chubby Charlie was not frightened of a rubber ball and he threw himself in front of it and made a spectacular stop.

"A good piece of play!" blared Uncle Mark.

The Sea Dogs were not to be deterred though; they continued the assault relentlessly with a barrage of shots. Chubby was undaunted. He became a piece of elastic and stretched himself to the limit to block the ball. Finally, Chubby stopped one with his soft seaweed pad and the ball bounced high in front of him. He swung his stick and hit the ball with the flat part of the picket. It sailed over the heads of all the players and bounced crazily in front of the opposite goal. The Sea Dogs' net minder was totally surprised and the ball hopped through his legs.

A tied game.

"A good piece of play!"

"No goal!" argued number four. "The ball was hit out of the air."

"The goalie was only clearing the puck," countered Joe Stead.

The dispute continued and Tacker was beckoned to make a decision. Toby reestablished his position atop of the rodney.

"A freak goal but a good one," declared Tacker.

As Tacker made ready to drop the ball again, he pointed to the sky. "There's not much daylight left in that sky. I'd say, next goal wins."

The players reluctantly agreed. The ball was dropped and the event became a furious battle of survival. Shortly, Sylvester Hicks got position of the ball for the first time in the game. A quick glance told him he was all in the clear, and he took off. Two of the Sea Dogs went in hot pursuit, but it was pointless because Sylvester was fast. He always dazzled the crowd with his swiftness; the problem was though, he had not quite mastered the art of stopping and was frequently involved in sensational collisions.

"A good piece of play," yelled Uncle Mark. "You got a break away, Sylvester — give it to her!"

The crowd could smell a victory and the cheers echoed off the Roaring Cove cliffs. Sylvester became aroused by the excitement and he accelerated like a streak of lightning. The sun was now low in the sky and there was a blazing reflection on the ice. Sylvester became blinded by the glare and veered off course. He was heading straight for the gut.* A tide perpetually runs through the gut. Consequently, this area of water never freezes over. By the time Sylvester realized he was headed for open water, it was too late. He

---

*A channel of water between two larger bodies of water.

was unable to stop. He hydroplaned for a good fifty-feet and disappeared into a foamy splash. His stick surfaced first; then Sylvester bobbed up like a harbour seal. The tide was running out, and he was quickly being swept out to sea. The animosities of the battle were ignored and the two opposing forces instantly sprang into action. Toby's rodney was up righted. With the Eagles on one side and the Sea Dogs on the other, it was glided over the ice and launched out into the gut. One player from either team jumped aboard and with the aid of the two goalie sticks, frantically paddled toward Sylvester. He was going down for the third time, when big number four plunged his arm underneath the water up to his shoulder and grabbed Sylvester by the hair of the head. Displaying his fisherman's skills, he flicked Sylvester out of the icy brine like a codfish and landed him in the bottom of the rodney.

"A damn good piece of play!" yelled Uncle Mark.

By the time the rescue was completed, the sun had dipped behind the hills and it was too dark to continue the game. A brief meeting was held and it was agreed upon to resume the game first thing in the morning. The Kellop Harbour players were to be put up. Uncle Mark, Toby, Aunt Daisy, Paddy Whalen, and I volunteered to take in players — Sylvester insisted that big number four was to stay at his house as a favour for saving his life.

That night, a bit of a time was held in the Orange Lodge Hall and the Kellop Harbour players were shown some Roaring Cove hospitality. Around about midnight when we came out of the hall, the weather was on. The wind was a gale force, and it was driving warm rainsqualls from the south west. The storm continued for three days and nights. When it ended, the ice on Roaring Cove Pond was gone. The game was rescheduled for next fall and the Sea Dogs went home.

It was just before Christmas and a hard frost sent Tacker to the pond to check the ice. He resolved that it was safe enough, and word was sent to Kellop Harbour. Because many of the boats were still in the water at that time of the year, the team was spared a long walk, and arrived in two punts. A quick meeting before the game confirmed that this was a continuation of the game started last spring and it was first goal wins. The crowd was anxious for a settlement and there was no one in Roaring Cove who did not show up for the game — even Reverend King was at pond side.

Promptly at ten o'clock, Tacker dropped the puck. Instantly, number four, the big fellow with the bushy red beard, threw all of his weight into a riser shot; the goalie had no chance to move, and it was an obvious goal.

"A good piece of play," shouted Uncle Mark.

The game that everyone had waited eight months for was over in a few seconds, and it was a decisive win for Roaring Cove. Yes, a decisive win for Roaring Cove — the reason being was because big number four was now playing for the Eagles. During the three nights that he had stayed at Sylvester's house, he had taken up with Sylvester's sister, Lucy. By July, it was realized that Lucy and number four were going to have number one. They were married in September and the young couple moved into Lucy's grandmother's house. Number four had become a resident of Roaring Cove and naturally played for the Eagles.

The Eagles had made us all proud. Canada too made us proud that evening because they played their hearts out and defeated the Americans for the gold medal. We all left Uncle Mark's house after a delightful and nostalgic evening of hockey. When we stepped upon his bridge, we could see by the soft light of the moon, the Maple Leaf flapping in the night air.

"I s'pose you'll keep her up now will you, Mark?" Walt asked, pointing to the flagpole.

"Indeed I won't," answered Uncle Mark. "As soon as the closing ceremonies is over — down she comes."

The Little Christmas Tree

"As I did stand my watch upon the hill, I looked toward Birnam, and anon, methought The wood began to move."
William Shakespeare — *Macbeth*

Everyone in Roaring Cove knows there is some little thing wrong with Base Dalton. The majority believe he has never been right because he was born without hair and has never grown any — anywhere. I maintain, though, that his dementia only began after he failed Latin in grade nine and suffered a nervous breakdown because of it. Whatever the reason, Base is a master of calamity. His father, Aubrey, states that Base simply does foolish things. Three times he has gotten himself lost in the woods. He went adrift on a pan of ice and had to be rescued by helicopter. He blew up the shed while converting the outboard motor from gasoline to propane. He ended up in the hospital with a split skull after he shot an arrow into the air and watched it all the way up, and then all the way down. He poisoned all the hens by lacing the scratch with moonshine, and, within a few weeks of receiving his driver's license, he demolished four vehicles and a porch.

His first driving mishap occurred only hours after passing his driver's test. Aubrey's house, you see, is stuck to the Roaring Cove Cliffs like a knot on a log. If you step out his front door, you end up on the road; if you step out the back, you end up in the salt water, fifty feet below. Consequently, he has constructed a high ramp on which to park his pick-up truck. In an attempt to park the truck by backing onto the ramp, Base hit the gas instead of the brake, shot over the end of the ramp and crashed in the beach. Base suffered a broken nose and the truck was demolished. The Mounties were quick to issue a ticket — backing while unsafe.

As a result of the first misadventure, Base began driving headfirst onto the ramp. One week later while backing onto the road, he banged into Mrs. Dorothy Taylor. There were no personal injuries, but Mrs. Taylor's new car was totally destroyed and the Mounties dispatched another ticket to Base — backing while unsafe.

After reaching the realization that it was illegal to back up, Base was left with no option only to park on the road. One night, after a frolicking time with the boys, he came home and forgot to secure the parking brake. The truck rolled down the hill and crashed into Albert Hicks' house. Truck number two was demolished and Albert's house was left without a porch.

After much negotiating with his insurance company, Aubrey was in possession of his third truck in as many months. Reluctantly, he permitted Base to drive the truck to Middleville to watch a hockey game. On the way home in the fog, Base struck a big bull moose on the Bakeapple Marsh Road. The moose was killed, the truck was destroyed and Base ended up in the hospital. It was from this accident that he acquired his nickname. You see, Base was christened Alphonse Jonas Dalton. Base is short for baseball. When Base hit the moose, he passed through the windshield and settled atop of the animal. His bald head was severely gashed on the broken glass and required hundreds of stitches. It didn't take the Roaring Cove crowd long to realize that his bald, stitched head somewhat resembled a baseball and this is what they began calling him. Baseball was shortened to Base; the name stuck and Base never drove again.

It was just a few days before Christmas of last year when I received a call from Base.

"Schoolmaster, can you do me a little favour?" he asked

"I will if I can, Base," I answered. "What do you have on your mind?"

"Father went to Middleville this morning — Christmas shopping. He told me to cut the Christmas tree while he was gone. I got a lovely one cut up in the spruce droke.* I wonder if you can come up and bring it home for me?"

Base had done me a few favours over the years, so I was happy to oblige him.

"Father will be some proud of me," Base said when I picked him

*A patch of trees.

up. "Father likes a nice Christmas tree, and I got the dandy one cut."

We topped the spruce droke, and Base instructed me to pull onto the wood cutting road. I drove this road for about half a mile before Base ordered me to stop. He jumped out of the car, crossed a small bog, and disappeared into the woods. He was gone for fifteen or twenty minutes; I feared that he had again become lost. By and by, though, I noticed this huge grove advancing across the bog. When it got closer, I could see that it was a giant, bushy spruce tree. Base heaved his weight against it and stood it up.

"Whatta ya t'ink of her, Schoolmaster? Beauty isn't it?"

"A bit large isn't it?"

"Father likes a big tree," Base responded.

"How are we going to get that home?" I asked, realizing it was senseless to attempt to insert it in the trunk.

"Lash her on the roof." Base directed.

This I did. But once I had, I realized the huge branches hung down so that the car doors could not be opened.

"Climb through the window," Base suggested. I did, but only to learn that the branches were flattened to the windshield and I could not see how to drive.

"I'll guide you along," Base stated.

"I'm not sure I trust your judgement, Base," I responded as politely as I could.

I climbed back out through the window and sized up the situation. "It will have to be towed," I announced. "I'll go home and get the utility trailer,"

"Naw, that'll take too long. We'll tow her as she is," Base remarked.

Before I knew it, Base promptly freed the tree from the roof of the car by cutting my new rope into four pieces. He took one of the shorter lengths and half hitched the tree to the bumper.

"Now," he said, "take her easy."

Cautiously, I towed the big spruce tree out the gravel wood cutting road, down the highway and through the narrow road of Roaring Cove. When I stopped in front of Base's gate, a crowd quickly gathered.

Uncle Mark said, "I looked out the window and I said to Mae, 'come quick and look, 'tis something strange comin' down the road.'"

Harold Buffett, who was familiar with the play, Macbeth, because he played one of the witches in the "come home year" concert, commented that he thought it was Birnam wood advancing Dunsinane Hill.

"Is that a Christmas tree, Base or have you started cutting bonfire boughs early?" asked Albert Hicks.

"A Christmas tree," responded Base, "father always liked a big Christmas tree. Father will be some proud of me."

"And how do you plan to get that thing in the house?" questioned Uncle Mark.

Base stood back, looked at the tree and at the front door of the house. He approached the tree and spread his arms as if he were going to embrace it. Maintaining this stance, he walked to the door and took a rough measurement. Base's expression confirmed the obvious and several of the men in the crowd laughed. Undaunted, Base raced into his father's shed and emerged with a piece of old cod net. Like a cowboy roping a steer, he wrapped the net around the tree and tied it tightly so that the branches folded neatly against the stem. To the amazement of all watching, he effortlessly pulled the netted bundle through the door and into the tiny living room.

"Dat boy is not stun, you know," observed Walt Churchill.

"And dat he is not," agreed Uncle Mark.

Most of the crowd agreed and all went to see the results of Base's clever manoeuvre. As they looked on, Base suddenly produced his pocket knife and slit the net, freeing the tree. It sprang to attention like the hairs on the back of a surly dog. Those inside the door were sent diving for protection. Albert's glasses were picked off his eyes and hurled into the hallway, Uncle Mark emerged with a big scratch across his face and the cat was sent screeching up the stairs. Lamps and furniture were toppled over and the three-dimensional picture of Joey Smallwood was flicked off the wall and sent crashing to the floor. The large bottom branches sought any possible opening. They sprang into the kitchen, up the stairwell, into the hall, out through the front door, and one smashed through the living room window.

When Aubrey arrived back from Middleville, the crowd was still assembled. "What's going on?" He asked.

"I got the Christmas tree, father," announced Base.

Aubrey did not respond. He went inside to inspect the situation. When he emerged, he walked directly to me and looked at the tow rope still attached to my bumper.

"I would expect as much from Base," he said. "But I thought you'd have better sense, Schoolmaster."

I could not respond. I simply got into the car and drove home.

I heard later that Aubrey and his family spent Christmas with relatives and got back into their house shortly into the New Year. It was not because of the damages caused by the tree, though. It was because Aubrey ordered Base to remove the tree from the house. Base went in with the gas-powered chainsaw, started it up and reduced the big tree to sawdust. The fumes from the exhaust penetrated everything and the cat was found under Aubrey's bed, dead from carbon monoxide poisoning.

"Doesn't surprise me," commented Uncle Mark. "Everyone in Roaring Cove knows that there is some little thing wrong with Base Dalton."

Jonas Pickett Strikes Again

"I said if you're taken short you keep away from the fruit. That's dirty." William Golding – Lord of The Flies

The renowned British novelist, William Golding once said that the shape of society must depend on the ethical nature of the individual and not any political system. Obviously, William Golding had never been to Roaring Cove because if he had, he would never have made such a statement. You see, the crowd from Roaring Cove are the best in the world and Roaring Covers have a reputation for hospitality and kindness, but if you pick us apart, you'll find individual qualities that are anything but ethical in nature. For example, Alfie Lambert is a notorious devilskin. Jonas Pickett, is the worse kind of a sleeveen. Sylvester Hicks loves to fight when he is drinking. Sam Whiffin would skin a louse to save a dollar, and extract the milk from your tea to get the upper hand in a deal. Mrs. Dorothy Taylor is a gossiping troublemaker who is forever challenging the status quo. Aunt Daisy Snelgrove is an insidious hypochondriac who is an absolute parasite on the healthcare system. Even Uncle Mark White, the most respected man in Roaring Cove, can be an impulsive cynic and, if you ask the right people I dare say you would find a fault or two with me.

If you look at us as a collective bunch, however, it's different. The actions of the group compensate for the behaviour of the individual. Therefore, Golding was amiss in his thinking. Our Community Charity Committee, of which all of the above are members, except Jonas Pickett, is a perfect example of this. Its mandate is one of benevolence, generosity and compassion. Just recently, for instance, the committee came to the aid of Lydia Blackmore, a young widowed woman with two small children, who lost her house to fire. The committee quickly organized a door to door collection and received contributions of used furniture, appliances and other household paraphernalia. She was temporarily housed in the basement of the church until a new house could be built for her. The men of the committee volunteered their time and began cutting logs so that construction could begin in the spring. Gideon Forward volunteered the use of his sawmill and he permitted the men to cut on his timber block and to stay in his old wood's cabin on the back of Bakeapple Marsh.

Everyone worked together and the men organized themselves into groups; one party cut and the other used their snowmobiles to haul the logs to the mill. At the end of each day the volunteers met at Gideon's cabin for a big scoff.* On Saturday nights the men would overnight in the cabin and have a bit of a time to celebrate their week's work. Paddy Whalen always brought along his accordion and there was never a shortage of moose stew and moonshine.

Although Jonas is not a member of the Community Charity Committee, when he heard about the good time the men were having at Gideon's cabin, he decided to get in on it.

He called Thumb-On Swyers, the chairman of the Community Charity Committee, "I'm not a member of the committee, but I'd like to help out with the logs for Lydia's house, so you can count on me for this Saturday," he declared. Thumb-On tried to discourage Jonas by assuring him that they had plenty of help, but Jonas insisted.

Saturdays were the days that I helped out and Jonas knew it. Therefore, shortly after three o'clock on Friday afternoon he showed up at the schoolhouse.

"Schoolmaster, is ya goin' in cuttin' with the boys tomorrow?" he asked.

"Yes," I answered.

"Would ya mind givin' me a ride? He asked. "I'm goin' in to lend a hand. I can sit on yer slide."

I reluctantly agreed, knowing full well that Jonas was the last person the men wanted to see at Gideon's cabin. Jonas is one of the individual types that Golding talked about — the type that possessed enough immoral qualities to tarnish the larger body, and I knew his motive. He would do little or no work, he would bring little or no

---

*A big meal.

provisions, he would eat and drink more than anyone else, and, if there was any way of spoiling the time, he would. I was right on all counts.

It was a clear, frosty Saturday morning and I arose with the sun. The hum of snowmobile motors echoed off the Roaring Cove cliffs as the other men made their way along the well-beaten trails. Hurrying to join the entourage of do-gooders, I swiftly jumped a snow bank in Jonas' yard and stopped only inches from his door. I raced the motor to announce my arrival. I raced it again…and again. Thirty minutes later he emerged remarking that his alarm clock didn't go off. He carried nothing only the clothes on his back — a well-worn one-piece snowsuit.

"Got no knapsack or anything, Jonas?" I asked.

"Nope," he grunted, "not stayin' all night."

The chain saws were already buzzing when I arrived at the spot where the men were cutting. When I pulled up, all eyes went to the figure of Jonas squatting on my slide like an ornament on a Christmas craft. As the slide came to a full stop, he let out a vicious groan and rolled into the snow.

"You hit a yes-mam* back there, Schoolmaster, and bounced me about three feet into the air. I landed hard on me tail bone and I got me back hurt."

I saw the whites of several of the men's eyes as they rolled them in disgust.

"I figured as much," tutted Uncle Mark.

"And I s'pose you won't be able to cut wood with a bad back," remarked Thumb-On with biting sarcasm.

"Wouldn't be a good idea," responded Jonas, oblivious to the ridicule — or not caring.

"I think you had better take me over to Gid's cabin, Schoolmaster, so I can rest up for a while."

I looked around for an answer.

"Go on and take him back," said Gideon, "and get him out of

---

*Dips in a woods trail - named for the nodding motion of the head that occurs when one rides over them on a slide.

the way."

I could hear the men grumbling as I turned my snowmobile around to head for the cabin. Jonas was rampant in pain by the time I arrived, and I had to lead him inside and help him into one of the bunks.

"Schoolmaster, I hope you got lots of personal liability insurance against yes-mam injuries. Old Jonas is likely to sue you for all your worth," Uncle Mark tormented when I returned.

"The thought had actually crossed my mind," I said.

"If he knew he'd get something out of it, he'd do it for sure," added Gideon.

When we finished our day of cutting and hauling, the sun had already set and the temperature quickly plummeted. The air was full of little puffs of vapour as the exhausted men exhaled into the still night and the snow squealed as each weary step compressed it. The pull cords of the snow machines had stiffened and the motors were reluctant to ignite.

"I hope old Jonas got a good fire roaring when we get to the cabin," Thumb-On interjected.

"I wouldn't place any money on that," rang out a voice from above the sputtering machines.

We found Jonas the way I had left him — still in the bunk. He was in fetal position with his one-piece snowsuit zipped up to his chin and his hood tied tightly over his head. He obviously had made no attempt to start a fire or to have done anything else.

Thumb-On pulled me to one side. "Now, Schoolmaster," he said, "you brought that good-for-nothing in here, so I'm trusting to you to take him home, so the rest of us can enjoy our evening."

Jonas appeared to be sleeping as we made preparations for the night. Gid and Paddy Whalen dashed off to the lake and retrieved a bucket of clean water for the kettle and the pots. Uncle Mark and I peeled and cleaned the vegetables and Sam Whiffen cut up the salt meat and prepared the moose. The rest of the men busied themselves securing firewood for what we knew was going to be a chilly night. When everything was prepared, the cabin warmed and the pot humming on the stove, Paddy set the mood with a jig on the accordion and Winse Hillard produced a jug of moonshine. Not to be outdone, Jobie Rodgers produced another jug.

As soon as the cork popped in the jug, Jonas sat up.

"Dat's the very thing needed to ease the pain in me back," he said.

If Jonas' back was bothering him, it didn't show in the spry way he hopped out of the bunk and dashed across the floor to the moonshine jar. He poured himself a hefty portion from Winse's jar and smacked his lips loudly as he took the first swallow.

Heeding Thumb-On's orders, I made my pitch. "When you get that drink gone, Jonas, I'll take you out."

"I don't think me back could take another ride on that slide today," he responded. "I 'low I'll have to put up for the night."

Nobody was surprised, and the whites of many eyes again flashed.

"The only thing is," he continued, "I didn't count on stayin' all night, so I didn't pack a lunch."

Then he scanned the room expecting someone to articulate the community sharing theory and say that there was enough for everyone. No one gratified him with the offer.

Jonas was undaunted, though, and he reached for Jobie's jar. "Now, I'll try your stuff, Jobie, and see if 'tis any better than Winse's."

He proceeded to drink freely, alternating from jar to jar. When the moose stew was served up, he was the first one to grab a plate.

"Your back seems all right now, Jonas," Uncle Mark teased. "Most of us who had been workin' all day couldn't lift what you got piled on that plate."

Jonas merely grunted and began his assault on his dinner with the table manners of a snowplough.

As he was ramming the last spud into his mouth, he was pouring himself another glass of moonshine. He continued to drink until the liquor ran out of the corner of his mouth and over his chin. And, as usual, the more he drank the more cantankerous he became, arguing with anyone who presented any opinion. He complained that Winse was putting too much wood on the fire, Paddy was playing the accordion too loudly, the moose stew had given him heartburn, and Lydia Blackmore should have carried insurance on her house. When he made some smug remark about Catholics, Sylvester Hicks, who also had a few drinks in, offered to separate Jonas' head from his shoulders. It took four or five of the fellows to restrain Sylvester, and the incident ended with insults and curse words being hurled across the floor.

Finally, around midnight, Jonas had reached the saturation point and made an attempt to walk to the bunk he had occupied all day. His coordination being somewhat impaired, he stumbled into the stove, knocked the funnel off its mount and he ended up in the wood box.

"Leave him there!" shouted Sylvester.

Thumb-On and Gideon scrambled to reposition the funnel before the cabin filled with smoke and Winse and I picked up Jonas and fired him into the bunk.

Instantaneously, he began to snore.

"He might not have cut any wood today, but it sure sounds like he's cutting it now," said Paddy.

Then, Paddy played several old-fashioned waltzes to drown him out while the rest of us played a game of cards. Gideon had just shouted thirty for sixty when Jonas sat up in the bunk holding his stomach.

"I got vicious cramps in me stomach," he said. "I gotta go to the toilet!"

"Make no wonder with what you're after puttin' in it," commented Jobie.

"Where's the outhouse at, Gid?" Jonas asked.

"There isn't one anymore," responded Gideon. "It fell down years ago. Had no need to rebuild it. You'll have to go down in the woods but make sure you go well back from the cabin."

Jonas pulled open the door and was hit by a solid wall of bitter, cold air. The icy wind whipped into the cabin, lifted the cards off the table and caused smoke to baffle from the stove. Jonas, quickly stepped back in, fully zipped his snowsuit and pulled the hood tightly over his head. Then he dashed through the door and disappeared into a veil of vapour. He left the door swinging.

"I hope he frost burns his backside," commented Sylvester as he slammed shut the door.

Jonas was gone for about fifteen minutes when he suddenly burst into the cabin panting for breath. His nose was blood red with the cold and his eyebrows were frosted white. He made straight for the jar on the table, filled a glass and went to the stove to warm himself. He unzipped his snowsuit and loosened his hood. Presently, a stench permeated the heated room.

"Who farted?" asked Gideon.

"Not me," chorused all hands at once.

Accusations flew around the room as each of us pointed the finger at the other. Eventually, our flaring nostrils settled on Jonas.

"You dirty sleeveen, Jonas! You're after shittin' in ya clothes!" shouted Sylvester.

A pitiful look of innocence came cover Jonas as he denied the charges. But the undeniable odour caused him to check himself.

"There's nothing on me," he attested.

Alfie and Paddy began to sniff at the air like two hunting dogs. They circled the room and simultaneously stopped in front of Jonas. Paddy was snorting and grunting like a beagle on a hot scent, and I thought he would break into a bark at any moment.

"'Tis you all right, Jonas" said Paddy.

"Lift ya boots," he ordered.

Both men checked Jonas' boots. His feet were clean but they continued to investigate. Suddenly, Alfie grabbed his nose and pointed to Jonas' hood.

"Blessed fortunes, Jonas...you're after doing a job in ya hood!"

The look of horror on the two men's faces beckoned us all to view the spectacle. Sure enough, the hood of Jonas' snowsuit was heavily plastered with, what was obviously, his own waste.

It was clear what Jonas had done. He had gone into the woods to relieve himself, dropped his one-piece snowsuit, like one would a pair of pants, and squatted into position. He heedlessly neglected to realize that the upper portion of the suit was crumpled underneath him.

Then it dawned on me that Jonas' hood had been up and securely tied when he reentered the cabin. I immediately looked at his head. His hair was matted with the substance as well. I felt the pit of my stomach begin to ascend and I swallowed hard. The other men became aware at about the same time as I did. The cabin emptied within seconds.

The reaction was mixed. Some of the fellows were heaving, others were cursing and some were laughing. The one thing we all had in common was that no one was going back inside that cabin.

"I'll freeze to death before I go back in there," proclaimed Gid.

"What're we going to do?" I asked.

"Pack it up and go home," Sylvester announced in a tone of disappointment.

"I knew it!" shouted Thumb-On. "I knew that slippery sleeveen would ruin our night."

Someone shouted instructions for Jonas to pitch out the articles of clothing that was left inside. He did so, and we all suited up and prepared to head home.

"What about Jonas?" I asked. "We can't just leave him."

"Yes we can," answered Sam.

"Well, you brought him in so you can take him out, if you're brave enough," Thumb-On remarked. "Just make sure I gets a good head start on ya."

I wasn't brave enough.

"Get yourself cleaned up, Jonas, and I'll be back for you sometime tomorrow!" I shouted above the roar of the snow machines.

It was well into the afternoon the next day before I arrived back at Gid's cabin. It was a clear, frosty day and I noticed that the smoke from the funnel was rising lazily into the still air.

"Well, at least he's not frozen to death," I muttered to myself.

The cabin felt warm and cozy as I opened the door, but once inside, that familiar aroma greeted me.

There was Jonas slumped over the table with Winse's

moonshine jar in front of him and Jobie's lying empty on the floor. I grabbed the birch broom from behind the door, stood my distance and poked him a few times just to make sure he was not dead. After a few sharp jabs in the ribs, he stirred.

"What're ya at Jonas?" I shouted in frustration.

He raised his head in a drunken stupor and incoherently mumbled something that I could not understand. Then his head fell back to the table.

"Stay here and freeze for all I care!" I bellowed in anger, and I immediately left the cabin, started my snowmobile and went home.

I did not bother with Jonas again and I thoughtlessly forgot about him. I know he made it home, though, because Aunt Daisy met him walking out on Manuel's Point. She stopped to speak to him and caught wind of what went on. She promptly made a visit to Dr. Templeman requesting a tetanus shot claiming she had caught lockjaw off Jonas Pickett. When Mrs. Dorothy Taylor learned about the incident, she blew the whole thing out of proportion by filling in details about Jonas having been poisoned. Sylvester vowed that the next time he saw Jonas, he was going to poke him in the chops for spoiling his time. Sam Whiffen made a special trip to Jonas' house in an attempt to sell him a new snowsuit and Uncle Mark was overheard saying, "Jonas is too lazy to muck* shit from a rooster over slippery ice."

Not one person in Roaring Cove had a good thing to say about Jonas. Nevertheless, at the Community Charity Committee meeting that week, we unanimously voted to include Jonas on our list to receive a Christmas hamper. The more I think about it the more I realize William Golding was wrong.

---

*To carry.

What's in a Name?

"My name, dear saint, is hateful to myself, Because it is an enemy to thee." William Shakespeare – *Romeo and Juliet*

A while back I had occasion to play the role of lawyer and I do confess it was a most interesting experience. It all started when I happened by the post office and learned about a fuss that was going on between two of our newest residents in Roaring Cove. Leander Jacobs and Obe Sampson came to Roaring Cove from Little Big Harbour earlier in the fall as a part of a resettlement agreement their community had made with the government.

Little Big Harbour is a tiny settlement about half way up the shore between Roaring Cove and Kellop Harbour. It was settled in the sixteenth century, and managed to sustain itself from the inshore cod fishery. However, when a cod moratorium was declared in 1992, the people were forced to rely on a government compensation package. When the fish did not return and the package ran out, many of its younger families began to move away. Little Big Harbour was left to the older folks and a few die-hards. The government quickly began reducing services and life elsewhere became an attractive option.

The community requested that government develop a resettlement plan. This was done and each household was offered a sum of money to move — $60,000 with an additional $2,000 for each dependant child. Obe and Leander vowed that no amount of money could replace a culture, but others thought this to be fair and voted to accept the proposal. Obe and Leander changed their minds when the ferry stopped running and the gas generators were shut down. They joined their friends and neighbours, boarded up their windows and doors, secured the cemetery plots, and uprooted four centuries of history. Soon, thick brogue accents permeated cities and towns far and near; and, people who routinely dropped in for a cup of tea, were now sending Christmas cards to one another. Little Big

Harbour was left to the gluttonous gulls. Obe and Leander minimized the upset by moving their families thirty miles down the coast to Roaring Cove.

Mrs. Dorothy Taylor, the Roaring Cove walkie-talkie, was in the post office that morning and she gave me the news that the two life-long friends were engaged in a bitter dispute and were no longer speaking to one another.

"It's all over the compensation package they received for moving," she announced.

"How come that?" asked Uncle Mark emptying the flyers from his mailbox into the garbage can.

"Apparently, Obe became jealous because Leander received more money than he did."

"Sure, the government decided what each family would get," Uncle Mark added.

"Yes," responded Mrs. Taylor, "But apparently, Obe has three youngsters and was entitled to $66,000 — which is the amount he received. Leander, on the other hand, has only one child and was entitled to $62,000 but received a cheque for $78,000."

"Then, 'tis the government they should be fightin' and not each other," added Albert Hicks.

"It seems that Obe blamed Leander for providing the authorities with misleading information," continued Mrs. Taylor, "and, Leander accused Obe of calling him a liar and the racket started from there."

Jonas Pickett who came in on the end of the conversation claimed that the people from Little Big Harbour should have stayed where they were. He maintained that he was living in isolation on Manuel's Point, and, as long as the government had money to throw away, they should pay him to move.

"There's skullduggery going on somewhere," added Paddy Whalen.

"And maybe it was an honest mistake," responded Albert.

"And maybe it wasn't," added Jonas.

The conversation got old Jonas, the biggest sleeveen of all times, thinking, and when he went home, he contacted the authorities and requested the same deal that the people from Little Big Harbour had been given. When he was refused, he informed the government that the whole program was flawed because Leander Jacobs had been overpaid to move to Roaring Cove.

This caused the government to launch an investigation and to realize that Leander had indeed been overcompensated. As a result, Leander was ordered to reimburse the government, and he was charged with a misdemeanour of fraudulent misrepresentation and summonsed to appear in court in Middleville. Leander, a shy, timid man was most distraught over the whole affair, and regretted the day he ever set foot outside of Little Big Harbour.

Now, I had come to know Leander well in the time he had been in Roaring Cove because his daughter, Nina, was a student of mine, and Leander took great interest in her education. Consequently, he came to me seeking help and advice.

"What will I do, Schoolmaster?" he asked.

"Simply tell the truth, Leander," I advised.

"I've never been in a courtroom before, and I'm not one for speaking out in a crowd," he confessed.

"Then, get yourself a lawyer," I suggested.

"That's more money than I can afford," he admitted. "I was wondering if you would consider speaking on my behalf?"

I was not anxious to get involved, and I had no particular knowledge of the law. I told Leander so.

"But you'd only have to give my side of the story," he pleaded.

"And what is your side of the story, Leander?" I asked.

"'Tis not much of a story to it. This man from the government came to my house, asked me some questions and wrote everything down in a big book."

"What kind of questions?" I asked.

Leander gave me the complete details of the interview, and it all became perfectly clear to me.

"Yes, Leander," I announced, "I'll proudly tell your story!"

News of the court case quickly circulated and it became the talk of the town. Obe was feeling terrible that his friend was in trouble with the law, so he apologized to Leander and the two resolved their differences. On the day of the trial, the tiny Middleville Court House was packed with a crowd from Roaring Cove.

"The case of the Crown verses Leander Jacobs!" blared the judge with a sharp rap of the gavel.

The formality of the scene and the seriousness of the situation hit me, causing my stomach to flutter, and my legs to weaken. I approached the bench like a henpecked husband who had gone on a drinking spree.

"Are you the counsel for the accused?" asked the judge.

"No, Your Honour. I'm the Schoolmaster."

"That much I know, sir, but are you representing the defendant?"

"I am here to tell Mr. Jacob's side of the story, Your Honour."

"Well then, please commence to do so, Mr. Schoolmaster."

Sensing intolerance in the Judge's tone, I abbreviated my prepared defence to one statement, hoping it would be sufficient. "There was no crime; it was all a misunderstanding, your Honour," I blurted.

"And would you care to elaborate for the court, sir?"

I turned to face the crowd. I saw Uncle Mark, Gideon Forward, Aunt Daisy, Toby Avery, and the rest of the Roaring Cove crowd — all familiar, friendly faces. Leander, his wife and daughter were sitting in the front seat, and Obe was sitting across from them. I relaxed and started in.

"Well, Your Honour, I feel it essential to explain to you that it is customary around our part of the coast to refer to people by names other than their given names."

"You mean, like a nickname?"

"Well, more or less, Your Honour."

"Continue please."

"Well, for example, Your Honour, the mayor of Roaring Cove is Theodore Swyers but everyone calls him Thumb-On-Wrench because he was born with a deformed left hand and because he is a mechanic by trade. And then there's Alphonse Jonas Dalton who is known as Base because his bald head resembled a baseball when it was stitched up after a car accident. We started calling him Baseball and then shortened it to Base."

"Does this have anything to do with the case before the court?" the Judge asked.

"Not directly, Your Honour, but these are important examples and there are other examples as well."

"There are?" The Judge sighed.

"Yes, Your Honour, there's the two Dan Malloneys, both exactly the same age with their birthdays on the same day but in no way related. We call one Red Dan and the other Black Dan."

"And why is that?"

"It's a little confusing, Your Honour, because Black Dan has red hair and Red Dan has black hair so one would think that it would be the other way round. The truth is, hair colour has nothing to do with their respective names. The names were given because both men bought their first pick up truck on the same day. Red Dan bought a red one and Black Dan bought a black one. Neither man has since changed the colour of his truck so we named them for this reason and it stuck."

"Yes, and Red Dan always buys a Ford and Black Dan always buys a Chev," shouted Paddy Whalen.

"Order please. Order in the court! Continue Schoolmaster."

"And then, Your Honour, there's the example of Kil Churchill. His real name is Miles but when we changed over to the metric system several years back, the community found it fitting to change Miles to Kilometre. Kilometre became shortened to Kil and there's hardly anyone in Roaring Cove would know who you were talking about if you referred to Miles Churchill."

"Bar Moore is another example, Your Honour. Bar was christened Heith Charles Moore, after the English doctor who delivered him. Now, Your Honour, you know as well as I do that the people of Roaring Cove don't pronounce *ths* and we are notorious for dropping *hs*. Consequently, Heith Moore became Eat Moore. Eat Moore is the name of a candy bar, Your Honour. Therefore, Heith Charles Moore became referred to as Bar Moore."

"Will you please sum up and make the point relevant to the

case, sir?" the Judge impatiently urged.

"Yes, Your Honour. The point is this. I have attempted to show the court that people around places like Roaring Cove and Little Big Harbour often change and shorten people's names."

"That you have done at great length, sir."

"Tell him about why we call Levi Baker Three Quarters," shouted Albert Hicks causing the courtroom to erupt in laughter.

The judge rapped his gavel hard. "Order…order in the court! Please spare the court any further elaboration, Schoolmaster, and begin your summation."

"Well, Your Honour, Leander Jacobs, his wife and their only daughter sit before you. Leander is charged with having committed a deliberate act of fraud. The truth of the matter is that Mr. Jacobs has no idea why he is before this court today. His only crime results in the fact that he named his only daughter after his poor deceased mother, Nina Jacobs, a well-respected woman who lived her entire life in Little Big Harbour. Just as Mr. Jacobs, for his entire life, had called his friend Obadiah — Obe; he also calls his only daughter, Nina — Nine. So, Your Honour, when the government agent interviewed the accused and asked if he had any children, Mr. Jacobs answered truthfully. He responded, 'Yes, I have Nine.' Now, Your Honour, the compensation for moving from Little Big Harbour was $60,000 per family and $2,000 for each dependant child. The agent wrote nine in the space allotted for number of children. Nine times two is $18,000, Your Honour, add that to $60,000 and you get $78,000, the amount Mr. Jacobs received for his resettlement package. It was all an honest misunderstanding."

A murmur went through the crowd. The Judge raised his gavel, but he did not drop it. He looked at Leander for a long time. His stone-like expression softened and he asked, "Mr. Jacobs, have you returned the overpayment to the proper authority?"

"Yes, Your Honour," responded Leander in a barely audible voice, "every penny."

"Very well then…case dismissed," the Judge bellowed punctuating his announcement with a knock of the gavel.

The Fires of Bonfire Night

"For the most wild yet most homely narrative which I am about to pen, I neither expect nor solicit belief. Mad indeed I would be to expect it, in a case where my very senses reject their own evidence." Edgar Allan Poe — *The Black Cat*

Roaring Cove, like most Newfoundland communities, has hundreds of stories about strange and inexplicable phenomena that have sent tingling sensations down the spine of a brave fisherman and have caused many a youngster to sleep with a blanket tucked securely between the pillow and the back of the head.

Most of these stories were handed down from a time when communities were isolated and winter nights were long. For entertainment, families visited each other and either played cards or told stories. Often the stories were flavoured with the supernatural and many a ghostly tale was told while heavily vamped feet were being warmed on oven doors. In Roaring Cove, however, the origins of many of these yarns can be traced back to the devilskin, Alfie Lambert.

For years, on foggy nights, a mysterious light could be seen drifting across Bakeapple Marsh. News of a jack-o'-lantern and a headless traveller terrorized the town and no one dared to venture far from home on such nights. On the night Margaret Rodgers gave birth to her daughter Sally, the fog had settled thick when Jobie set out for Dr. Templeman by way of Bakeapple Marsh Road. He summoned the doctor to come quickly and started back alone to be with Margaret. As he approached the marsh, he noticed a strange light following him. The glow pursued him almost to the bridge where it crossed in front of him and disappeared into the foggy night. More concerned about Margaret than he was for himself, Jobie refused to alter his course. Dr. Templeman was following closely behind and, as he approached the bridge, bumped into Alfie carrying an old ship's lantern. The jack-o'-lantern has not been seen in Roaring Cove since the night Sally Rodgers was born.

An equally terrifying tale was the one of the sailor's coffin that would appear on Gut Bridge — the bridge over the channel that connects Roaring Cove Pond and the ocean. Rumour has it that on nights when the moon was full, the coffin of a drowned sailor floated in from the ocean and became wedged between the water and the underside of the bridge. If a foot traveller dared to cross the bridge at this particular time, the coffin would ascend and claim the poor soul. On several occasions students from the east point, on their way home after a school dance, were denied access to the bridge because of a hollow thumping sound of a coffin coming from underneath it.

One night when the entire school body was decorating the gymnasium for its graduation ceremonies, Toby Ivany observed that the tide was ebbing on a full moon. "A fine night to stab a lobster or two" he thought, so he secretly tapped the rocks around Gut Bridge in an attempt to poach a meal of the tasty crustaceans. Just before midnight, he noticed Alfie rowing across the harbour in his dory. He rowed his dory up to Gut Bridge, and hid away underneath it. Knowing full well that it was Alfie's intention to frighten the young students, Toby met them as they left the schoolhouse and alerted them. The boys in the group quickly devised a plan. They cheerfully began marching over the bridge. When the thumping noise sounded underneath them, the boys pretended to freeze in apparent fear. Then, the entire group ceremoniously urinated over the bridge and down through the planks. The muffled sound of cursing rumbled out from underneath the bridge and the sound of the boys' laughter echoed over the harbour. The thumping coffin has not been heard since.

There was another time when a dark figure came out of the cemetery and accosted Aunt Daisy Snelgrove on her way home from a Friday night bingo game. There was no doubt in Aunt Daisy's mind who the mysterious character was because she recognized the black raglan he was wearing as one that had belonged to old Chappy Lambert, Alfie's grandfather.

The story I am about to relate occurred on bonfire night, a night celebrated with bonfires and pranks, held to commemorate Guy Fawkes' effort to burn the British Parliament Building in 1605. When Alfie was younger, he brought terror to Roaring Cove on this night. He routinely cut down clotheslines, unhinged gates, flattened tires, and exploded firecrackers in people's porches. And, sometimes he took things beyond what people in Roaring Cove called harmless mischief. One year he set fire to Jonas Pickett's outhouse. That might not have been terrible, given the dilapidated state of the thing, except for the fact that Jonas was in it. Another bonfire night he robbed Paddy Whalen's rooster from the hen's pound and hoisted the squawking cock full mast up the flagpole on the Fisherman's Hall. And, another time when the town was aglow with the bonfires, he set fire to a bag of horse manure on Sam Whiffen's front step, prompting Sam to stamp it out with his vamp feet. Now that Alfie is a young man, bonfire nights have been reduced to a few cut clotheslines and a lot of roasted potatoes. Nevertheless, I cannot say with any degree of certainty if he, or anyone else, had any involvement in the events of this particular bonfire night.

The wind was strong and was tripping from north to northwest causing it to whine mournfully through the loose classroom windows that were not yet sealed with plastic for the winter. Scattered snowflakes had been falling all day and were being whirled wildly by the wind before they settled on the muddy ground turning underfoot into a dirty, slippery mess.

The wind had a sedative effect on the students and they stared blankly out the windows while the baseboard heaters cracked and squeaked in tune with the serenading wind. The heaters had been turned on for the first time since the previous spring and a collection of summer dust burned to fill the classroom with a stale, musty smell similar to that of a root cellar or any other unventilated place. Some students expressed a concern that they would not be able to start their bonfires on such a night and the issue developed into a discussion on Guy Fawkes and British democracy.

Suddenly, the sound of the church bell invaded our little classroom and blended with the other foreign sounds. It was not the slow tolling of the bell soliciting parishioners to a service, but an abrupt and unsettled clang. It meant only one thing — an emergency. The children stiffened in their seats and glared at me inquisitively.

"I'll try to find out what it is," I announced and I made my way to the staff room telephone. As I passed the front entrance, I noticed Reverend King's car pull into the schoolyard. He left the engine running and ran inside. He was panting for breath when he entered and his face was pale with a troubled expression. His long greying hair, which was usually parted above his left ear and swept over his crown to conceal his balding, was thrown askew by the wind and his white scalp shone through. He looked aged and fatigued.

"The little Pearce boy is missing!" he proclaimed.

"But he's only a baby," I added.

"Twenty-six months."

The child to whom Reverend King was referring was the son of Annie Pearce, a young, unwed woman who had moved to Roaring Cove from Kellop Harbour while in the latter stages of pregnancy. Social services moved Annie into an old rental unit that had been floated in from Manuel's Point and mounted on stilts against the hills with barely enough room for the road to sneak between the front door and the edge of the cliff. Shortly after Annie's baby was born, Alfie Lambert took up company with her and Mrs. Dorothy Taylor and others began to talk.

"I want you to organize a search," Reverend King requested.

"What about the classes?" I asked.

"Dismiss them," he replied. "You can use the older children in the search party."

Reverend King was chairman of the School Board and had authority to dismiss school whenever he felt a situation warranted it. I was in no position to argue with him, and the children were jubilant when I cancelled school.

Snow continued to fall and heavy, dark clouds were tumbling low over the Roaring Cove cliffs when I arrived at the house of the missing boy. A handful of men with collars turned up against the wind moiled around the road in front of the house, unsure of what to do. Annie was alone. There were no women with boilers of soup to support and comfort her. She met me in the doorway. Her face was flushed and her dark eyes stared not at me, but straight through me. Her movement was slow and awkward and when she spoke her words were thick and dry. She darted her tongue over her lips in an attempt to moisten them.

"Thank you for coming, Schoolmaster."

"What happened, Annie?" I asked.

"It's my little Joey; he's gone — disappeared."

"How long has he been missing?"

She paused and twisted her hands in her apron before responding. "Since sometime after breakfast."

"Have you looked throughout the house?"

"A dozen times," she responded.

"And where was he when you last saw him."

"In the living room."

I swept my eyes past Annie and looked into the house. She simply stood dazed.

"Show me!" I snapped.

Startled out of her reverie, she stepped to one side, ushered me into the house and led me directly into a spacious living room. A chesterfield, covered in a multicoloured, crocheted afghan, and an old-fashioned oil space heater was the only furniture in the room. The well-worn canvassed floor was scattered with children's toys. An archway on the far wall opened into a long narrow hallway, and a set of stairs descended from the second story and stopped short of a front door.

"He was in here," she choked. "I sat him on his potty and went into the kitchen for only a few minutes and when I came back there was no sign of him." Suddenly, Annie fell to her knees and looked underneath the chesterfield. "It's gone too!" she shouted. "His little potty is missing too!"

"Where's Alfie?" I asked.

"Gone in the woods," she replied, "left before daylight this morning."

My mind raced for an explanation. "The child must be hiding," I concluded.

"Are you sure you've looked everywhere? Is there any place he could have tucked away?"

Annie simply shrugged her shoulders and threw open her arms in a gesture of despair. As she did, I placed my hand on the front door knob and unconsciously turned it. The door flew open into the road. I looked questioningly at Annie.

"That was locked," she said. "I always keep it locked."

I immediately turned my attention outside. A few more men had congregated and several of the school children were racing up the road toward the house. "It looks like the boy has gone outside, check all around," I shouted. As the men dispersed, I jumped upon a splinter of rock that projected from the cliff, cupped my hands over my face and called Joey's name. The wind indignantly carried my voice into the cliff where it was lost. A lone raven perched high on the bluff mockingly squawked back at me.

The search turned up nothing and one by one the searchers meandered back to the house with their hands in their pockets. Hayward Green voiced the opinion that was on the minds of most. "That devilskin, Alfie Lambert is behind this."

"Alfie has been in the woods since daylight," I interjected.

Harold Buffett said what the rest of us refused to think. "I think the boy has gone over the bank and into the water." We walked across the road to the cliff's edge and looked over. Harold rubbed his foot over the ground. "Slippery underfoot too," he added.

I was immediately struck with a horrifying vision — that of a young child floating face down in the frigid water. I saw a tiny body being pulled into a punt, and a tiny coffin being lowered into the ground.

When I shook myself back to reality, I noticed that Uncle Mark had joined the crowd. I asked him, "What do you think? Could he have gone over the cliff?"

He deliberated only long enough to wipe a drip from the tip of his nose with the back of his hand. "Well, if he is, it's a body we're looking for, and you had better get the boats in the water before dark. If he's anywhere close by, he'll show up."

"That makes sense," I commented. Of course Uncle Mark always made sense. "Divide into two groups," I ordered. "One group continue to search the community, and another drag the harbour." I decided to help with the dragging operations.

By the time I got to the wharf, two boats were already launched and outboard motors were being fastened in place. A drag net that had been kept in some twine loft especially for this purpose was being assembled between the two boats. Meticulously, we scoured the harbour, running parallel to the cliffs, stopping frequently to check the net. Winse Hillard was commenting that the day was beginning to close in when the church bell once again rang out. I intuitively cast my glance skyward, up the grey granite cliff. At its edge, a lone black figure stood silhouetted against the dark sky. I recognized him as Reverend King by the incongruous white collar against the otherwise dark scenery. He was swinging his arms motioning us ashore.

"They must have found the boy," bellowed a voice from the other boat.

Only a few students were at the wharf when we landed. "The little boy is found!" one of them shouted.

"Where?" sounded several voices at once.

"He was in the house all the time. Alfie came home from the woods and found him in the living room."

A grumble went through the crowd but only Sylvester Hicks was vocal. "What in the hell are we doing out here? Is this another of Alfie's bonfire jokes or what?"

Sylvester didn't wait for the boat to touch the wharf. His temper was at the boiling point. He placed one foot on the gunwale and jumped, clearing a good six feet of water and landing on the dock. He was in a fighting mood. "This time Alfie Lambert has gone too far and when I gets me hands on 'em he'll bloody well know it!"

81

It was Uncle Mark who calmed Sylvester by asking, "would you rather we had found the boy drowned, Sylvester?"

I did not help secure the boats, but went straight to the house and entered the way I had left — through the unlocked front door. Reverend King and Annie were sitting on the chesterfield: Alfie was standing, holding little Joey in his arms.

"Alfie, you had better have a good explanation for this or Sylvester Hicks will make away with you!"

"I don't know what's going on!" he responded. "I hurried out of the woods when I heard the church bell ring for the second time. I ran in the house to see what had happened and Joey was sitting right there on his pot."

I turned my attention to Annie. "Annie, I have the whole community in an uproar. I even had men dragging the harbour."

"My baby is safe, that's all I know," she sobbed.

"Reverend King?" I implored. He looked at me without expression and held up the child's pot.

"Well," I beckoned.

"Look."

"It's a piss pot — so what?"

"It's not the same," he responded.

"Not the same, how?" I demanded, my impatience obvious by my intonation.

Reverend King squirmed uncomfortably and made hand gestures in an attempt to make me understand what it was he was saying. "It looks like a photograph negative of the original."

My puzzlement was obvious and he continued. "Look. It's a white enamel pot; or, it was a white enamel pot with dark spots where the enamel was chipped off. Now it is reversed — the black spalled spots have turned white and the rest of the pot is black."

I have to admit that I found the whole thing rather amusing and I reached down and took the pot from Reverend King. Much to my surprise it was icy cold. "Alfie," I said, "this has been outside."

Before Alfie could respond, Reverend King snatched the pot out of my hands. He produced a white silk cloth from about his person and wrapped the icy pot in it. "Now there will be no more talk about this, "he said. "We can't explain what happened here today, so I see no need to alarm the community. There will be enough gossip as there is." Then he bid us all a good evening and he left with the little white bundle tucked under his arm.

I immediately started in on Alfie with a barrage of accusations. He completely ignored my allegations and made no attempt to defend himself. Instead, he placed little Joey in Annie's arms and proceeded to comfort her. I left the house feeling as frustrated as I did when I entered it.

Outside, it was dark. The air was heavily laden with smoke from the dozens of bonfires that already had been lit. From around the place, flames leaped into the darkness and flankers* showered skyward each time green, spruce boughs were added to the infernos.

That night I was haunted by the events of the day, so sleep did not come easily. One minute I was awake and aware while the next I was suspended in a zone between consciousness and unconsciousness holding an icy pot in my hands, searching a net, and fighting with Sylvester Hicks and Alfie Lambert. All the time the church bell was ringing. Suddenly, I sprang awake and realized that the bell was no dream. For the third time that day it was ominously resounding through Roaring Cove. I ran to the window and threw open the curtains. The night sky was illuminated in an orange glow, and I could see thick black smoke ascending into the night air. I knew this was no bonfire.

I dressed quickly and headed in the direction of the fire. Shortly, heat from the blaze was scalding my cheeks. There was no saving the manse; Reverend King had escaped with nothing more than the clothes he was wearing.

The next morning a crowd sifted through the charred tangle, searching for anything worth salvaging or for a possible cause of the fire. Most believed it was a spark from a bonfire, but Reverend King was not of that assumption.

"Look what I found!" shouted Alfie Lambert and he rooted the

*Sparks from a wood fire.

pot from among the smouldering remains. It was charred black but otherwise intact. Alfie picked it up and brought it to Reverend King and handed it to him. He accepted it as though he was taking a hot plate from off a stove. The good Reverend's glasses slipped down his nose and his jaw sagged. "It's still icy cold," he whispered. Alfie smirked, gave us a wink and a nod and walked away.

The Like was Never Before Known

"You are the only young man that I know of who ignores the fact that the future becomes the present, the present the past, and the past turns into everlasting regret if you don't plan for it!" Tennessee Williams – The Glass Menagerie

Well, the like was never before known in Roaring Cove. The sleeveen, Jonas Pickett told Sam Whiffen to go straight to hell. He cursed on Alfie Lambert and told him to crawl away somewhere and perish. A big bull moose swam across the harbour and landed on Manuel's Point. There was an unseasonable rain storm followed by a deep freeze and a heavy snow storm. Alfie and Sam went missing and Jonas began attending church on a regular basis. As strange as it may seem, all of these things are related.

It all started one Friday afternoon in Sam's shop. I was picking up a few groceries and Alfie Lambert was picking up some beer. Suddenly, Jonas burst through the door. Heavy rain had been falling all day, and Jonas was soaking wet and puffing and blowing like a diesel motor on a frosty morning. He totally ignored Alfie and me and stepped up to the counter.

"I wonder if you'd cut up a bit of moose for me, Sam?" he asked.

Sam paused and furrowed his brow before replying. "Moose this time of the year? Where did you get the moose this time of the year?"

Jonas stammered and shrugged his shoulders. "A feller gave it to me," he answered.

"I don't know of anyone who got moose to be giving away." Sam muttered.

"'Twas a feller from up in Kellop Harbour," Jonas snapped.

The blood splattered on Jonas' face told us where the moose came from. Everyone knew about the moose that swam ashore on Manuel's Point and the thick fog that accompanied the heavy rain offered perfect cover under which someone could perform an illegal act.

"Are there any tags on it?" Sam asked.

"I don't think so," Jonas answered.

"Then, I can't cut it up," said Sam.

"And why not?" Jonas insisted with a hint of irritation.

"Because I could get in trouble," Sam responded.

"How can you get in trouble by cutting up a bit of moose?" Jonas grunted, growing red in the face.

"Because it is illegal to be in possession of poached moose meat — that's why," said Alfie Lambert wading into the conversation.

"You shut ya mouth Alfie Lambert!" Jonas snapped.

Jonas' temper was now at the boiling point and he turned to Sam and pointed his finger in his face. "So, you're tellin' me, Sam Whiffen, that if I brings in a bit of moose, you won't cut it up fer me!"

Sam squared his shoulders and stood his ground. "That is exactly what I am saying, Jonas Pickett!"

"Well, Sam Whiffen, you can go straight to hell!" Then Jonas turned and began to storm out of the shop.

I hid behind the biscuit boxes because I had learned a long time ago not to get into a fuss with Jonas Pickett. Alfie Lambert, the devilskin, on the other hand, was in his glee and pounced on the opportunity to have a bit of fun. Now, everyone in Roaring Cove knows the story about the last time Sam butchered a moose for Jonas. Jonas had obtained a license that year, and he delivered the moose to Sam with tags intact. Sam asked Jonas if he preferred the meat cut mostly into roasts or steaks. Jonas responded that he wanted both, and also some hamburger meat, sausages and a few pork chops. Alfie knew the story all too well.

"How do you want it butchered, Jonas? In pork chops or do you want a few chicken legs this time?" Alfie teased.

Jonas stopped suddenly and turned to Alfie with a glare that could have stopped a clock.

"Alfie Lambert...Alfie Lambert," he punctuated each syllable by tapping his index finger on Alfie's chest, "why don't you go crawl away somewhere and perish?"

Then, old Jonas stepped into the pouring rain and slammed the front door with such force that it shook the biscuit boxes.

"That's one miserable man!" Sam remarked.

Sam's comment launched us into a lengthy discussion about Jonas. It ended in a consensus — Jonas was more to be pitied because he wasn't the sharpest hook in the trawl tub.*

Alfie and I left Sam's shop together. The rain had stopped and the temperature had plummeted turning everything into a slippery sheet of ice. By dark, a fierce snow storm was bombarding Roaring Cove. Soon the lights and telephones fell victim as the strong winds caused the ice encrusted wires to snap like pieces of thread at the end of sewing needles. Wood stoves crackled and kerosene lamps glowed as entire families congregated in cosy kitchens. Within a few hours the roads were plugged and Roaring Cove took on a nostalgic ambience of isolation.

The next morning, the storm still raged and the town was in a panic. It wasn't because of the storm, though, it was because Sam Whiffen was missing. Penelope, Sam's wife spent a worried night thinking her husband was overnighting at the shop as he did sometimes during a storm. With the telephones out of order she could only assume. However, when morning came, she sent Paddy Whalen to check.

Paddy expertly manoeuvred his snowmobile through the high snow drifts to Sam's shop. It was locked securely, and there was no sign of Sam or his car. He checked all of the obvious places — the Legion Club, the church, Nelson Hyde's house — before sounding an alarm.

Soon a crowd of men on snowmobiles congregated and a search was organized. The town became a hum of buzzing motors but there was no sign of Sam. Everyone was mystified. A missing person was one thing, but a missing car as well was quite another matter. Finally, Uncle Mark White stepped forward with a theory.

"Sam's car is not very big," he said, "maybe it got stuck and is drifted over."

---

*A sawed off wooden barrel in which trawl lines are coiled. A trawl line is a partially submerged line to which shorter hooked lines are attached.

This was a plausible explanation, so broom handles, hockey sticks, and poles of every type were grabbed, and every snow mound from Bakeapple Marsh Road to the bus turnaround was poked and prodded. Several garbage boxes, two wood piles and a doghouse were all that was found.

Suddenly, Walt Churchill, the fire chief who was more or less in charge of the search, sped his snow machine in among the searchers, jumped upon its seat and made an announcement that complicated the whole situation.

"Men," he shouted, "I have just been informed that Alfie Lambert has not been seen since yesterday."

It was common for Alfie to stay out all night, so his mother was unconcerned until Alfie didn't show up for dinner. After hearing that Sam Whiffen was missing, she sensed something was wrong and raised an alarm. Alfie's buddies, Joe Stead and Art Pearce, were quickly contacted. Neither had seen Alfie, so he too was officially registered as missing.

Was it possible that Alfie and Sam were together? Everyone agreed this most unusual. Alfie and Sam weren't exactly companions. Could Sam have offered Alfie a ride home in the storm? I confirmed that Alfie left the store the same time as I did. Was it possible that he returned? Everyone was shouting suggestions and offering opinions; there was confusion and much panic.

Uncle Mark stood up and demanded attention.

"All right men," he said, "first of all we must remain calm. There is a logical explanation for this, and we will find it."

"Yes," shouted Hayward Green sarcastically, "Sam's car is buried in a snow drift."

Uncle Mark was undaunted by the comment and he continued. "There are not many places two people and a car can disappear in a place the size of Roaring Cove. The roads are blocked so they couldn't have left town even if they had wanted to."

"What are you getting at, Uncle Mark?" Walt Churchill asked.

Uncle Mark lowered his head and scuffed his boot in the snow as if contemplating a life or death verdict. "We all know how slippery it got yesterday when it turned cold, so we have to assume the worse." Uncle Mark stated.

All eyes immediately turned to the water and the high cliffs. Uncle Mark had said what no one else wanted to.

Immediately, a group was sent to the government wharf to engage a boat to search the waters lapping at the ballicatters.* For the rest of the afternoon, men who knew every rock on the harbour bottom searched the shoreline where the road runs along the top of the cliffs. And, much to the relief of everyone, they turned up nothing.

Darkness left the community in bewilderment, so Walt Churchill called a public meeting.

"I want every man, woman and child to meet in the schoolhouse at nine o'clock in the morning," he announced.

Few slept easily in Roaring Cove that night and the kitchen fires burned long as neighbours gathered around wood stoves conjuring up fascinating stories of tragedy, carelessness, felony, and even fairies.

The next morning the schoolhouse was packed to capacity. Walt Churchill stood before the people.

"Ladies and gentlemen, you all know why we are here today. And, as your fire chief, I would like to be able to tell you I have a plan. However, I am at a total loss, so I have to call for suggestions from the crowd."

Before anyone had an opportunity to respond, the door swung open and Jonas Pickett entered. A collective sigh went through the crowd, and an awesome silence fell over the room. Creaks and groans in the old wooden structure that usually went unnoticed were disturbingly audible as Jonas walked straight to the front of the room and spoke directly to Walt.

"I got news on Sam Whiffen and Alfie Lambert," he said.

Walt's jaw dropped and his eyes opened. "You have?" he asked. "Where are they?"

"They're dead!" Jonas responded abruptly.

---

*A thick strip of ice-encrusted rock or shoreline caused by constant freezing spray or waves.

Another sigh went through the crowd and my heart jumped into my throat when I recalled the disagreement that Jonas had with the two missing men.

"Dead!" Walt enunciated.

"Yes, dead!" Jonas confirmed.

"How?" Walt asked.

"I don't know how," Jonas answered.

"Then, how do you know they are dead?" Walt appealed.

"Because they spoke to me." Jonas retorted.

This comment caused another murmur to go through the crowd, and Jobie Rodgers spoke out. "How can they be dead, if they spoke to you, Jonas?"

"Don't mind Jonas, he's gettin' on with his trash again," someone bellowed from the back of the room.

"I tell you Alfie and Sam spoke to me from the beyond," Jonas confirmed.

"Now we know he's off his head," someone else shouted.

"Hold on now," Walt ordered. "Give him a chance to explain." Walt pulled over a chair and gave it to Jonas. "Here Jonas, sit down and explain yourself."

Jonas squatted on the chair, cleared his throat and began. "Well, the crowd from Kellop Harbour knocked down that big bull moose that had been hangin' around the woods on back of my place and one of them offered me a quarter off it."

"Crowd from Kellop Harbour, my arse." Sylvester Hicks interrupted.

"Be quiet Sylvester and let him finish. Go on, Jonas, finish your story," Walt encouraged.

"Well, this morning I went to where the moose was," Jonas continued, "and as I walked up to it, it spoke to me. And it spoke in the voice of Alfie Lambert. It came to me as plain as anything. It said, 'Jonas...Jonas...help me...it's me...Alfie.'"

"Smell his breath, Walt and see if he's been drinking," Paddy Whalen shouted from the back of the room.

"I swear to God I didn't have a drop of anything today," Jonas pleaded. "And I swear to God it was Alfie's voice, but it was the dead moose that spoke."

"Dat's Alfie up to his old tricks again," Paddy Whalen yelled.

"What happened next?" Walt encouraged.

"I don't mind sayin', Walt. I got one awful fright. So I got out of there as fast as I could. I made straight for town by cutting down behind the dump. Then, as I was passing the dump, Sam Whiffen's voice echoed out of the sky to me."

Paddy shouted another comment. "He might not have been drinking but he's on drugs."

"Sam's voice, too?" Walt queried.

"Yes, Walt, 'twas Sam's voice and he said the same thing Alfie said. He said 'Jonas...Jonas...help me. It's Sam.'"

"And why do you think Alfie and Sam are dead?" Walt asked.

"Because I had a fallin' out with the two of them on Friday." Jonas sought me out in the crowd and pointed to me. "The Schoolmaster was there; he can vouch for that. And now they have come back from the dead to haunt me."

Things weren't making much sense but, for the first time in two days, Walt felt as if he had a lead. The dump is at the end of the road and Manuel's Point, where Jonas lives, is beyond that — there had to be a connection.

"Did anyone search the area around the dump and out on Manuel's Point?" he asked.

Some of the fellows confirmed that they had circled the dump several times and had seen nothing. No one, however, had been to Manuel's Point.

"You have to take us to where you heard the voices, Jonas." Walt insisted.

"I want to see Reverend King," Jonas demanded.

Jonas was adamant and only after meeting with Reverend King and arranging for him to accompany us did Jonas agree to take us to the spots where he claimed to have heard voices.

The school house emptied, and Walt, Reverend King and Jonas, led us on a pilgrimage to the northeast side of town — to the dump and to Manuel's Point. What was astounding about this trek was that most had arrived at the schoolhouse by snowmobile, but no one selected to use them. Instead, we all walked in single file and in sombre silence. I hurried to the front of the line for fear of missing something.

The storm had blown over and it was a breathtaking winter's morning. The sun danced on the fresh snow drifts and Roaring Cove looked like a soft tea cake settled in whip cream.

When Jonas reached Roaring Cove Beach, he followed his tracks in the snow and led us up Sailor's Hill. From the top of the hill we had a complete view of Manuel's Point and the dump.

"The moose is in there behind the yellow marsh, in that droke of young spruce," he pointed. "I heard Sam's voice somewhere around about here."

He continued to follow his tracks down the other side of the hill when suddenly a voice echoed from out of the stillness. The entire procession stopped like an army that had been commanded to halt. The silence was deafening. Then the voice came again.

"It's me…Sam…help me…help me!"

All eyes turned skyward.

"Here for God's sake. I'm down here!"

The voice was hollow and tinny and it resonated through the air, but there was no mistaking it. It was Sam Whiffen's voice.

"There," pointed Walt Churchill. "It's coming from down there."

When the voice came again, all located it. It was amplifying from the mouth of the teepee shaped garbage incinerator. As if given the order to charge, an army of Roaring Covers descended on the site. Within minutes the most spry among us were looking down into the rusty incinerator. Sam Whiffen, white-eyed and smutty faced, was standing atop of his car looking back up at us.

Thumb-On-Wrench quickly jumped over the platform, ran down behind the structure, and unhinged the metal clean-out door freeing Sam. An applause went through the crowd when Sam surfaced.

Uncle Mark, as considerate as always, looked at young Bobby Hicks who was standing next to him. "Go tell Penelope we've found Sam and he's ok," he ordered.

Sam quickly erased the curiosity that was painted on the faces before him by explaining what had happened.

"I threw a couple bags of garbage into the trunk of the car when I closed up on Friday," he said. "It had turned cold and it was slippery, but I didn't think it was as slick as it was. When I backed onto the incinerator ramp and touched the brake, the car didn't answer at all. Before I knew what was happening, it slipped through the incinerator gate, broke through the safety chain, and ended up in the bottom of the incinerator among the burned out garbage. Try as I might, there was no way I could climb out."

"You were some lucky the incinerator wasn't fired up and burning," Thumb-On interjected.

Reverend King looked at Sam and said with sympathy, "you look like you've been to hell and back, Sam."

"That is exactly where I have been," Sam answered, and he glared hard at Jonas who was standing next to the Reverend.

"I didn't mean it, Sam!" Jonas blurted. "Really I didn't!"

"Sam, have you seen Alfie Lambert?" Walt asked.

"Not since Friday afternoon," Sam answered.

Walt knew that his mission was not completed so he turned to Uncle Mark.

"Uncle Mark, take care of Sam," he ordered. Then he ordered Jonas to continue on to where he had seen the moose.

Most selected to stay with Uncle Mark and Sam. Jonas agreed to continue only if Reverend King came along. I helped drag the Reverend across the snow-covered marsh to the spruce droke.

Suddenly Jonas stopped, "there," he pointed.

Lying dead before us, was a big bull moose. We stopped and looked from one to the other. Then, as if given some secret order, we simultaneously sneaked toward the thing. When we were but a few yards away from it, we heard a pitiful groan.

"It's not dead!" shouted Walt, jumping back.

"Looks stiff enough to me," I added.

"I can guarantee it's dead," Jonas added.

"I'm not dead," the muffled voice sounded.

"Who is it?" Reverend King asked. "What do you want?"

"It's me...Alfie...for the love of God get me out!"

"'Tis the devil himself," Jonas shouted. "He's come to punish me."

Suddenly, a line of oaths began to rumble from the moose. There was no mistaking it. It was Alfie Lambert's voice, so Walt and I cautiously approached. Upon closer inspection we could see that the moose had been partially butchered and was certainly dead.

Walt lifted his foot and kicked the moose hard in the ribs. "Is that you Alfie?"

"Yes, 'tis me."

"What do you want?" Walt asked.

"I want to get out of here," came the reply.

"And exactly where are you?"

"I'm in the moose. For heaven's sake, get me out!"

Immediately, it hit me. I knew exactly what had happened. I fell to my knees and began to dig away the snow that had drifted around the moose's torso. Within seconds I could see the jagged incision where someone had chopped open the moose to paunch* it. I stuck my fingers into the cut and tried to rip it open, but it was frozen shut.

"Give me a hand, someone."

Instantly, Thumb-On grabbed a starrigan* that was leaning against a tree, stuck it into the cavity and threw his weight on it. With a crack the chest cavity broke open and like Macduff, who from his mother was untimely ripped, Alfie tumbled out onto the snow. Wide-eyed and bloody-faced, he smiled up at us.

"What in the world are you doing in there, Alfie?" Reverend King asked.

"One of Grandfather Lambert's old tricks," he replied.

I knew that Alfie was referring to the story about his grandfather, Chappy Lambert, who got caught in a snow storm on the high country while moose hunting and survived by crawling into the belly of the moose he had just cleaned.

---

*To remove to stomach of a butchered animal.
*A small evergreen tree cut for firewood or for fence railings.

"I crawled in to get shelter from the storm, and was comfortable enough until I tried to get out and realized the moose was froze together." Alfie explained.

"But what were you doing out here in a storm?" Reverend King inquired.

"I followed Jonas to where he had poached the moose thinking I'd hack off a fry or two."

"I didn't poach a moose," Jonas interrupted.

Alfie glared hard at Jonas with raised eyebrows and the rest of us smiled.

"Before I knew it, the storm was ragin', and I couldn't find the path. If you fellars never came when you did, I would have perished in there."

"You crawled away and nearly perished," Jonas blurted. "God help me. I'm cursed!"

Jonas turned to Reverend King and in one breath explained how he had told Sam Whiffen to go to hell and Sam fell into the incinerator. Then he confessed to having told Alfie Lambert to crawl away and perish and Alfie nearly suffocated after crawling into a moose.

I had never seen Jonas so distraught. He went on and on begging forgiveness and he urged Reverend King to exorcize him. It took three or four of us to escort him to his house, and we poured several good drinks of moonshine in him before he settled down.

Well, Sam and Alfie soon got over their ordeals, but Jonas is still convinced that he somehow wished doom upon Sam and Alfie, and after what Jobie Rodgers did to him last Sunday coming out of church, he's not likely to recover any time soon. You see, since all of this happened, Jonas, for the first time in his life, has been attending church. Jobie Rodgers came up to Jonas, after the morning service and said, "So Jonas, have you cursed anyone lately?"

Temporally returning to his old self, Jonas shot back, "drop dead Jobie."

Jobie grabbed both hands to his chest, let out a painful grunt, and fell to the floor.

"Oh blessed fortunes!" Jonas shouted. "I've done it again," and he took off through the door and down the road. No one has seen him since.

Mr. Black Pun Hump

"But, the extraordinary homeliness of her gait and manner would have superceded any face in the world. To say that she had two left legs, and somebody else's arms, and that all four limbs seemed to be out of joint, and to start from perfectly wrong places when they were set in motion, is to offer the mildest outline of the reality." Charles Dickens – *The Battle of Life*

He was the most diminutive of men. He stood about five feet nothing and could have balanced a quintal* of fish on a seesaw. The angles of his slight frame were sharp and geometrical making him look like he was built from driftwood by an unimaginative child. His face was his most sharp feature and can best be compared to a cliff of rock that had been assaulted by an angry sea. His cheeks were deep eroded gulches and his nose and kingcorn* were splinters of sharp granite rock rising from an expressionless sea. He spoke in a high, squeaky voice, and he emitted little sprays of spittle each time he enunciated the *p* sound. He would grow red in the face and the sinews in his neck would bulge and pulsate when he became nervous or excited — which was often. He epitomized clumsiness and often did and said things that defied logic. By Roaring Cove standards he made Base Dalton look normal.

He came to Roaring Cove from somewhere off the island – the mainland or the United States. No one knew exactly where and no one grew close enough to him to ask. When Roaring Cove got its new school and the children were bused in from all the smaller places up and down the coast, we were told by a school board demigod, who had been sent here to deliver us from the depths of ignorance, to expand the curriculum. If our children were to amount to anything and become anything but fishermen, they were to attend the one and only government-sponsored university. In order

---

*A unit measurement for weighting fish. It equals 112 pounds.
*Adam's apple.

97

to do so, a foreign language was required. Latin was looked upon as old fashioned; so, considering we were a part of a great dominion with two official languages, French was the choice of the day. Teachers of French, however, were as rare as dentists were and one was found only after an appeal went out via some overseas publication. Hump was the result of the search.

His name was Jeremiah Edward Mills. His nickname, Black Pun Hump is rather unique and the story behind how he got it is well worth the telling. The "Hump" part of the name was given to him because of Uncle Mark's innate ability to coin a metaphor and Alfie Lambert's ability to promote mischief. You see, Hump's centre of gravity seemed too high for his puny frame. When he walked, he perpetually stumbled forward while making quick little steps as if trying to catch up with his shadow. The first time Uncle Mark laid eyes on him, he said that the chap somewhat resembled a crackie* trying to hump a soccer ball. Alfie Lambert, who was within an earshot of Uncle Mark's comment, thought the analogy was appropriate and somewhat funny and quickly labelled the new French teacher, Hump. The nickname went through the school like an epidemic of head lice and stayed with Jeremiah until the day he left Roaring Cove.

Now, if Hump were in any way offended by his new name, he should not have been. Students in Roaring Cove, and students everywhere I would suspect, are notorious for decorating their teachers with creative appellations and it is done so without intent of malice. As new teachers came to our little school, they were promptly nicknamed. Hump was not alone.

Whereas Hump acquired a part of his name because he was uncoordinated and awkward when he walked, Mr. Robert Gilmore obtained his because his walk was rhythmical and harmonious. Robert strutted around lifting and lowering his arms and legs like the pistons of a precisely timed machine. Teddy Rodgers, who had started picking apart motors when he was six years old, labelled him Four Stroke. It was also Teddy who named Mr. Eric Dunne

---

*A small frisky dog.

Dipstick because he stood more than six feet tall, was straight as an arrow and weighed about 125 pounds. And, the names were not always given because of physical appearances. Mr. Russell was called God because he taught Religion. Mr. Marsh was affectionately referred to as Mr. Bog, and Miss Sarah Smallwood was called nothing only Miss Splits* and the list went on. I shudder to think of the titles bestowed upon me over the years.

Mr. Lambert Hynes came to Roaring Cove at the same time as Hump. Lambert was a pleasant gentleman and as fine a mathematician to have ever circumscribed a triangle. Now, Lambert had been in a serious accident when he was a young boy — the details of which he shared with no one. As a result of the accident, Lambert had major facial disfiguration and one of his eyes was much higher than the other one was. Penny Green, the brightest student ever to come out of Roaring Cove was a history buff and most fanatical about Greek Mythology. She took one look at Lambert and called him Cyclops, after the tribe of one-eyed giant monsters described in Homer. Although most of the other students had no knowledge of Homer or the lawless cave-dwelling Cyclops, the name sticks to this day. In spite of Lambert's facial deformity, however, he was, at the time, youthful and possessed rugged, handsome qualities and every available girl in the place — and according to rumours, a few who were not as available — were cracking their necks over him. Lambert, though, was not interested. His heart was pledged to Becky, his high school sweetheart back in the city. When he returned to Roaring Cove after the Christmas break, he came back with Becky as his new bride. Hump, who never attracted attention from any of the ladies — available or not — jealously remarked that Lambert had his eye set on a city girl all along. Hump was most notorious for unintentionally blurting out comments like this that often belittled serious situations. When Dipstick taught his English class that a pun was, "a humorous play on two words having the same meaning or similar sounds but different meanings,"

One student quickly said, "Like Mr. Hump does."

---

*Kindling.

Consequently, Pun became attached to Hump and Mr. Hump became known as Mr. Pun Hump and he well earned it.

When our school had an outbreak of scabies, commonly known as the itch, the public health nurse called an after school meeting and named the infected students. After the meeting, Hump claimed that the epidemic was far worse than the nurse realized. He maintained that she had only scratched the surface and he was itching to tell her so, but he didn't want to offend her.

One day I was sitting at my desk when Hump burst into my office. His face was crimson, the veins in his neck were clearly visible and he showered me with spittle as he hyperventilated with excitement.

"What seems to be the matter, Mr. Mills?" I asked.

"That Alfie Lambert is up to his nonsense again."

"And what is it this time?"

"He's jammed a wad of chewing gum inside the clock in my classroom!" Hump shouted.

"And this is what has caused you to become so upset?" I asked in a calm tone, trying to settle him down a little.

"Yes it is," he retorted loudly. "My patience is stretched to the limit, the time is stuck on three o'clock and I am totally ticked off. And, I expect you to do something about it!"

"What would you like me to do?" I inquired.

He pointed his tiny, bony finger straight at me and responded in a tone of accusation. "You're the Headmaster, so I expect you to give him a good chewing out and make him do time in detention."

When a student put a thumbtack on Hump's chair and Hump sat on it, he reprimanded the whole class telling them that he saw no point in such immature antics. Other examples of his puns include: He caught wind of the fact that some of the boys were having farting contests in the back of his classroom, he thought that Dipstick went a bit overboard for taking three hours to show his class the movie, *Titanic* and he insisted that teachers in trade schools, teaching courses like Cosmetology, had it easier than high school teachers because they didn't have to give make-up exams. One day, he stood up in a staff meeting and told Clarence Pine, the district superintendent that the school board was overstaffed and inefficient. "Mr. Pine," he said, "I want to make this point perfectly plain, as far as I am concerned, there is far too much dead wood in your board." Hump was forever complaining that his salary was too low; so, when the women's government workers sued for pay equity, Hump maintained that they were the only ones with balls.

As awkward as Hump was, he liked to tinker with things and try to fix them. He often did more harm than good, but at least he tried. He was in Roaring Cove but a few weeks when he bought an old jalopy from Thumb-On-Wrench Swyers. The first time he took it out, he got stuck in the mud on Bakeapple Marsh Road and ripped off the muffler, tail pipe and all the parts in between. For most of the night he stayed up lashing everything back in place with wire. The next day he showed up late for work claiming that he had overslept because he was exhausted. It was this fascination with fixing things that resulted in Black being prefixed to Pun Hump, and Mr. Jeremiah Edward Mills becoming known as Mr. Black Pun Hump. It started one day when Chubby Charlie Freak broke the new ping-pong table at school. We teachers were eating lunch in the staff room when a knock came upon the door. It was Chubby Charlie holding up the leg of the table in two pieces.

"I sat on the table and somehow it broke," he admitted with a sense of guilt.

"'Tis no wonder with the weight of ya," Cyclops whispered for Charlie not to hear.

Now, Charlie was a good boy and we all knew that the incident was an accident; most would not have reported it. Consequently, I saw no need for reprimand. "That's all right, Charlie — don't you worry about it. I'll get Winse Hillard to come in and fix it," I assured.

Suddenly, Hump came to his taps, stuffing food into his mouth. "That's all right, he said, no need for that. I'll bolt down my sandwich, and I'll fix it with a few screws."

Hump fixed it all right; he whacked four or five metal screws through the leg, on either side of the break. Then he tightened them to the bottom of the table so that the heads protruded through the top like night crawlers in wet grass. Later that afternoon, Chubby Charlie planked his fat arse back down on the same table and opened up a gash on his backside that took seven stitches to close.

I called Winse Hillard to come in to fix the table.

Hump watched with interest as Winse skilfully whittled down a mop handle, jammed it into the two hollow pieces of the leg and rejoined the break. Small holes were drilled through the metal leg and tiny screws were inserted to fastened the leg tightly to the mop handle inside. A little electric tape was added and the job was completed — stronger than ever.

"Well, well," said Hump. "You've got that problem mopped up, Winse."

This, of course was not exactly the incident that caused Pun Hump to be called Black Pun Hump; it was what he had learned from observing Winse that caused the extra appendage to be added. You see, Hump was renting the little bungalow that was next door to Aunt Daisy Snelgrove. Aunt Daisy was thrilled with the company and often brought Hump homemade bread, jams, and a scattered meal, to give her an opportunity to complain to someone. This day, Aunt Daisy was complaining that her sinuses were bothering her. She had them drained several times in the past, but she maintained that the problem kept coming back. She was certain that her current problem was being caused by the fact that her kitchen stove was smoking. Hump, wanting to return Aunt Daisy's generosity, and always willing to grab any opportunity to fix something, offered his help.

The next morning Aunt Daisy did not light her stove, so it was well-cooled off when Hump arrived to check things out. He lifted the dampers and removed the grates. Immediately, he could see that the stove was clogged with soot.

"Holy smoke!" he commented, "it's almost completely blocked off, 'tis no wonder it wasn't drawin'."

"I'll have to get someone to clean it out for me I s'pose," Aunt Daisy hinted.

"No need for that. I'll do it for you," Hump enthusiastically offered. "Get me your vacuum cleaner. And you'd better put a clean bag in it — there's a lot of soot in there."

Aunt Daisy did as requested and Hump went to work like a professional. He cleaned the interior components of the old Waterloo stove down to the bare metal. Then he removed the funnelling all the way back to where it joined the brick chimney and gave it equal attention. "It's a wonder you didn't have a fire, Aunt Daisy. Even the funnels are full."

Next, Hump inspected the brick chimney itself and noticed a fair build up of smut and creosote. "I had better get some of that out of there too," Hump added. He proceeded to push the metal wand of the vacuum cleaner into the hole, bending it slightly so as to insert it further up the chimney. Suddenly, the wand snapped; Hump pulled it back and stood holding it up like a broke off breech loader.

"Oh my!" Aunt Daisy gasped.

"That's all right, Aunt Daisy — not to worry — I can fix it. Do you have an old mop handle around anywhere?"

"You might find one out in the shed." Aunt Daisy responded.

Hump disconnected the hose from the vacuum and went into Aunt Daisy's shed. There he located an old, dried up tar mop. Swiftly, he sawed off the handle and, following Winse's technique of repair to the last detail, he repaired the broken wand. Proudly, he returned to the house and showed Aunt Daisy his workmanship.

"Here you are, Aunt Daisy, stronger than it ever was. Now I can finish the cleaning," he said.

Hump reattached the hose and started up the machine. Unfortunately for Hump, and for Aunt Daisy also, he inadvertently connected the hose to the outlet end of the vacuum cleaner. That would not have been a serious problem, if it were not for the fact that Hump had completely blocked off the pipe with the mop handle. Now, the vacuum sucked air in, and there was no way for it to escape. Hump thrust the repaired wand back into the chimney and continued to clean, thinking he was doing a fine job. The vacuum groaned and strained. It became hot and swelled up. Suddenly there was a bang. The sides split apart and the pregnant bag exploded. Smutty, black soot showered into the air penetrating every crevice of the room. The white cat, Fluffy disappeared somewhere. It showed up two days later but remained black for weeks after. Aunt Daisy and Hump, looking like two coal miners, ran outside to safety. Jonas Pickett, who was on his way from Manuel's Point to pick up his weekly groceries, saw them and crossed to the other side of the road to avoid them. When he entered Sam Whiffen's shop, he inquired if there was a foreign boat in port because he had seen two black people outside Aunt Daisy Snelgrove's house.

Any person who has ever burned a fossil fuel knows that soot has a way of perforating the pores and Hump was still black around the eyes and behind the ears when he showed up for work Monday morning. His teeth gleamed white when he smiled — which wasn't often — and the whites of his eyes stood out like the beacon on Western Head Rock. As soon as the students saw him and learned what had happened that was it — his nickname was complete — Mr. Black Pun Hump. He took his name with him when he left Roaring Cove at the end of his first school year, claiming that he was not at all suited for this remote and rural way of life.

Hump was never to return to Roaring Cove and only once did anyone hear from him. Dipstick, of all people, received a note in a Christmas card a few years back. Dip read the note aloud to the rest of us. The year he had spent in Roaring Cove had made him realize that he wasn't cut out to be a teacher. He mentioned that he had been drifting around from job to job and place to place and was currently employed as a vacuum cleaner salesman.

"As long as he's not repairing them," Four Stroke muttered.

Then Dip began to laugh uncontrollably. "What is it?" I asked. He handed me the card and pointed to Hump's closing comments.

It read, "I thought teaching was bad, but this vacuum cleaner business really sucks. I don't expect to be at it much longer."

Cleanliness is Next to Godliness

"Ladies bathed before noon, after their three-o'clock naps, and by nightfall were like soft teacakes with frostings of sweat and sweet talcum." Harper Lee – *To Kill a Mockingbird*

The story that I am about to disclose is somewhat sensitive and private in nature and it is with a degree of reluctance that I share it. I do so only because Aunt Daisy herself, the main character in the plot of the story, has been going around Roaring Cove divulging even the most intricate details about the episode. It all revolves around the fact that Aunt Daisy is a hypochondriac who displays all the obvious – and some not so obvious – symptoms of this affliction, particularly an obsession with cleanliness and personal hygiene. She has been known, for example, to bathe several times a day when the weather is hot, and it's a candid fact that she frequently soaks her dentures in Javex. It was this obsession, and a little intervention from Alfie Lambert, that caused Aunt Daisy to be the victim of extreme embarrassment on a trip to the hospital one day earlier this summer. It was I who drove Aunt Daisy to the hospital that day, so I acquired the facts of the story first hand.

"You'd think she'd be ashamed to tell it," Aunt Mae commented after I told her and Uncle Mark my account of the happenings.

"She'd do anything for a bit of attention, even disgrace herself," Uncle Mark added.

"Well, everyone knows that Daisy Snelgrove is touched,"* Aunt Mae added.

"Yes, and touched a lot," Uncle Mark confirmed.

The story really began just before Christmas. The fish plant had been operating part time only, and many of the men received too little work to qualify for the pogey.* Consequently, the younger fellows, Alfie Lambert and his gang, went picking apples in Nova

---

*To have some degree of mental incapacity.
*Employment insurance.

Scotia. Uncle Al, Aunt Daisy's husband, went along with them. This was most unusual because Al had been retired for several years and had no real need to work and wasn't eligible for pogey anyway. The boys figured he went to get a well-deserved break from Aunt Daisy and most likely they were right.

It was well up toward Christmas when the work ended, so the men went on a shopping excursion at a giant mall that made Sam Whiffen's fish plant, the largest building in Roaring Cove, look like an outhouse. The men decided it was best to stick together, but somehow, Uncle Al got separated from the crowd, and they spent the best part of an hour looking for him. They found him in a little boutique that specialized in personal hygiene and health products.

"Well, you're certainly in the right spot to find something for Aunt Daisy," Joe Stead commented.

"What'll ya get her anyway?" Kil Churchill asked.

"I have no idea what to get," Al responded.

"Here, get this," Alfie Lambert suggested, holding up a bottle of bubble bath and a scrub brush.

"This bottle of vitamin pills won't go astray," Art Pearce teased.

Al beamed with pride as he counted out the money for his purchase — a bottle of Musk Oil perfume and a can of scented, talcum body powder.

"I can't wait to tell Aunt Daisy what you got her for Christmas," Alfie tormented. And, the devilskin of all devilskins, did not stop there with his mischief. That night, back at the boarding house, Alfie anxiously waited for Uncle Al to go to bed. When the older man began to rattle the headboard with his snoring, Alfie, certain that he would be undetected, sneaked into the bedroom and removed the can of talcum from Uncle Al's suitcase. He carried it into the kitchen like a rat stealing a spud from a root cellar and dumped the entire contents of the can into the garbage bin. Then, he meticulously refilled the can with flour, returned it to the suitcase and bragged about his cunning and skilful act to the other fellows.

Aunt Daisy, of course, was thrilled with her husband's thoughtfulness and tucked her present away for another day. That day came on that fateful trip to the hospital earlier this summer.

Aunt Daisy had been complaining to Dr. Templeman about certain women's problems, the specifics of which she openly shared with anyone who would lend her an ear. I will suffice to say that Dr. Templeman believed that there was some validity to Aunt Daisy's complaint and sent her off to the hospital in Middleville to see a specialist in such matters. Maybe, he did so to save Aunt Daisy, and himself, the discomfort of doing such an examination. In any case, Aunt Daisy's hypochondria emerged with a vengeance. She was convinced that her body was infected with some horrible disease that was spreading throughout her entire system, and she called Hayward Green to secure a plot in the old cemetery — in no way was she to be buried in that new spot under the hill — there was no view and the ground was soft. She developed a nagging cough and her voice became weak and hoarse.

"I'm not long for this world, you know. I can't be treated by Dr. Templeman so he's sending me off to Middleville because I'm a special case," she whispered into the telephone to Mrs. Dorothy Taylor, knowing full well that Dorothy would burn up the lines spreading the news.

When the time came for Aunt Daisy's appointment, she spent the best part of the previous day soaking in the bath. She did dry off long enough to wash the clothes she was to wear and pin them on the outside clothesline. Then she took it in, gave it a second wash and dried it above the stove, in case it had been subjected to any foreign pollutants or odours.

The next morning she was up before dawn, bathed twice more and packed an emergency kit in which she placed, pills, makeup, washcloth, soap, etcetera — and Al's Christmas present.

It was a hot and dusty ride over the Bakeapple Marsh Road, and, by the time we reached the hospital, Aunt Daisy was sniffing at her armpits. After another hour waiting in the overcrowded clinic, she was convinced that the smell of perspiration that was permeating the air was coming from her. It was bad enough to be showing herself to a complete stranger. She would be clean at least; so, off she went to the washroom to cleanse herself. There, she filled the sink with hot water, completely undressed, and, using the washcloth and soap from her kit, gave herself a full and thorough sponge bath. Still not convinced that her personal hygiene was what it should be for such an examination, she decided to spruce up a little. Again she reached into her overnight bag and pulled out Al's Christmas present — still in the gift bag. Without hesitation or thought of the consequence, she liberally doused herself in Musk Oil. Aunt Daisy walked into the clinic waiting room smelling like Penelope Whiffen on a Saturday night at the Legion Club dance.

Within minutes of sitting back down, Aunt Daisy's skin began to itch and a deep burning sensation invaded the most sensitive parts of her anatomy. She grew red in the face and began to hyperventilate. She twisted and turned on her chair in an attempt to become comfortable. Finally, she could stand it no longer; she jumped to her feet clutching herself, and screaming out in pain. Immediately, the nurses ran to Aunt Daisy's assistance and rushed her into the examination room in a wheelchair. The doctor was called in immediately.

She was a foreign doctor, obviously from some Asian country by her appearance — Japan or China. Aunt Daisy did not know which and she did not care. She was just happy that it was not a doctor she knew, and she was a female.

"You appear to be in some distress, Mrs. Snelgrove. What seems to be the problem?" she asked in a very thick accent that Aunt Daisy had difficulty understanding.

"I'm all afire, my dear — from the stuff I put on meself," Aunt Daisy answered in a Roaring Cove accent that the doctor had difficulty understanding.

"You applied something to your body. Is that what you are telling me, Mrs. Snelgrove?"

"Yes, doctor."

"And what was it, Mrs. Snelgrove?"

"Musk Oil, doctor. I put on some Musk Oil."

"Mush Oil," the doctor repeated unable to enunciate the hard consonant sound at the end of the word. "What exactly is this Mush Oil?"

"Stuff Al gave me for Christmas, doctor — to make me smell nice."

"I need to see this product, Mrs. Snelgrove, to determine its chemistry. Do you have it with you?"

Aunt Daisy reached into her little bag and pulled out the bottle which was now mostly empty. "Here it is, doctor. He got it on the mainland — I s'pose 'tis not poison is it?"

The doctor took the bottle and examined it. She smiled softly and handed it back to Aunt Daisy. "No, Mrs. Snelgrove, it is not poison — nothing a good soaking won't cure."

"What's wrong with her?" the nurses asked when they were instructed to prepare a cold bath for Aunt Daisy and to keep her in it for an hour.

"She applied *Mush Oil* to herself," the doctor replied.

The entire nursing station broke into laughter, but the doctor did not understand why.

"This water is freezing," Aunt Daisy complained as she climbed into the tub. "I'll end up with pneumonia."

"It's what the doctor ordered," the nurse responded. "The cold will take away the itch and the irritation."

The nurse was right. After twenty minutes or so Aunt Daisy was feeling fine and begged to be let out in fear of freezing to death. Nevertheless, she was required to endure the full treatment.

When she did emerge from the frigid water, she was as purple as Reverend King's cloak on Easter Sunday. She quickly climbed into the warm hospital gown that had been laid out for her, and she began to fix her hair and prepare herself before reentering the examination room. Intuitively, her thoughts went to her emergency kit and Al's present. She quickly located the gift bag and removed the can of talcum powder. This time she was more cautious; she held up the can and read the label:

> *Sprinkle powder all over and feel refreshed.*
> *TO USE: apply after bath or shower.*

Leaves skin feeling smooth and scented.

"Safe enough," she concluded. "I should have used this in the first place." She removed the hospital gown and generously sprinkled her still damp body with the contents of the can. Immediately, the white powder, or flour, began to curdle like sour milk in a cup of strong tea, and it clung to her body in clumps.

"Good heavens, good heavens," she cried. "What in the heavens is Al tryin' to do to me!"

Aunt Daisy tried to wash away the gooey substance, but the water caused the lumps of flour to swell even more. She was trying to pick the lumps off herself, one at a time when the nurse called out to her.

"Are you all right in there, Mrs. Snelgrove. We're ready for you."

When Aunt Daisy exited the bathing room, the look of distraught embarrassment was obvious.

"What's the matter, now?" one of the nurses asked.

"Oh, my dear," Aunt Daisy responded. "I'm all full of little doughboys."

All the nurses snickered, but the doctor did not understand why.

As it turned out, there was nothing physically wrong with Aunt Daisy, only some minor psychological scarring caused by embarrassment. Nevertheless, she proudly told her story and justified her actions by saying, "cleanliness is next to Godliness, you know."

The Young Ones

"... and I remember my youth and the feeling that will never come back any more – the feeling that I could last for ever, outlast the sea, the earth, and all men; the deceitful feeling that lures us on to joys, to perils, to love, to vain effort – to death; the triumphant conviction of strength, the heat of life in the handful of dust, the glow in the heart that with every year grows dim, grows cold, grows small, and expires – and expires, too soon, too soon – before life itself." Joseph Conrad – *Youth*

I cannot help but wonder what happens to people when they get older. The entire adult population of Roaring Cove has its drawers tucked up too tightly because a few youngsters have been riding all terrain vehicles and snowmobiles on the roads.

"Video games and television got them all drove off their heads," said Mrs. Dorothy Taylor. "They're taught no manners and they're spoiled rotten with expensive toys."

"They're all on drugs – dat's the trouble with the little buggers," alleged Jonas Pickett and Aunt Daisy agreed with him.

"One of 'em will end up gettin' killed or will kill someone else," Thumb-On-Wrench Swyers declared.

And the condemnation doesn't stop there. Reverend King has been preaching that the children of Roaring Cove are staying away from church and behaving in inappropriate and reckless ways. Last Sunday he said a special prayer for them and requested that the congregation be more diligent in tending to its flock.

Now, I have been the Schoolmaster in Roaring Cove for a very long time and I have known a lot of young people. It is my belief that the young folk of today are angels compared to what they were years ago, and those who are doing all the complaining now had better check the hooks at the end of their own lines.

Take Thumb-On, for example, he's adamant that the youngsters are endangering the lives of the entire lot of us. Yet, to the best of my knowledge, there has been one, and only one, snowmobile accident in Roaring Cove and it happened to none other than Thumb-On himself. He demolished an expensive snow machine and ended up in Middleville Hospital for several days. Apparently, he and Walt Churchill went ice fishing on Three Mile Pond far in the country behind Bakeapple Marsh. It was a brutally cold day with a fierce northern wind and drifting snow so the two fishermen kept on their snowmobile mittens while attending the wet lines. When they left to come home, Thumb-On bragged to Walt that his new machine was the faster of the two and challenged Walt to a race to the bottom of the pond. On the count of three, the race was on! Thumb-On's electric start machine jumped to the lead while Walt was still hauling the pull cord. Thumb-On grasped the throttle and squeezed it tightly; his aerodynamic machine cut through the frigid air like a harpoon. Almost instantly his two wet mittens froze solidly to the handlebars and to the throttle. Walt was half way down the pond when he met Thumb-On coming back. Thumb-On desperately yelled something when the two passed, but it came to Walt like a sonic boom and was lost in the roar of the machines. Walt stopped and watched as Thumb-On circled the pond several times, and he noticed Thumb-On ducking his head in an attempt to seek the shelter of the windshield. It was obvious that Thumb-On's face was beginning to freeze. Finally, Thumb-On could stand the bite of the wind no longer, and he noticed a spot on the side of the pond, where the small trees had caused the snow to drift into a high bank. He would drive into the snowbank, bog down the machine until it spun itself out and stopped. It was good logic, if it had worked. It didn't. The machine broke through the drift like a runaway snowplough, cleared an elongated path through the trees, and came to an abrupt stop in a large birch tree. Luckily, Thumb-On missed the tree, but he was projected into the woods another fifty feet or so. Only his feet were sticking out of the snow when Walt found him.

With three broken ribs, a fractured collar bone, and a severe concussion, Thumb-On need not worry about one of the youngsters killing him; he's quite capable of doing that himself.

And, as for Jonas Pickett and Aunt Daisy saying that the young ones are all on drugs, well, that's about as hypocritical as a politician chastising a schoolboy for lying. Aunt Daisy has been lugging around a purse full of pills for as long as anyone can remember. There's pills for rheumatism, pills for ulcers, pills for water trouble, pills for menopause, pills to put her to sleep, pills to keep her awake, and several for her bad nerves. Her husband, Al, says that Aunt Daisy takes that many pills that she rattles when she walks down the steps. Now, I don't think Jonas Pickett takes pills, but he sure consumes copious amounts of alcohol. Over the years, Jonas has absorbed enough home brewed beer, dog berry wine, and moonshine to float a punt and enough Beef Iron Wine to sink it. Before liquor stores, Beef Iron Wine was a connoisseur's delight. It is a pleasant tasting, blood building, tonic that contains about 30 percent alcohol. Sam Whiffen classified it as medicine and stocked it by the case; Jonas allowed that his blood was low and drank it in equal amounts. The one and only time that Jonas went for a physical examination, Dr. Templeman cautioned him that if his iron got any higher he would turn rusty. Now, I'm not right up on the young crowd's recreational habits or their substance of choice, but I'm willing to bet it's no worse than what is in Aunt Daisy's purse or what Jonas has been consuming all these years.

If drugs are not the problem with the young ones, then Mrs. Dorothy Taylor must be right and it must be the way they are raised. Well, I was raised by God-fearing parents in the time when sex was dirty and marriage occurred only within one's own denomination. Nevertheless, when I think back to my innocent boyhood, I have to question if our fun was all that wholesome and healthy. We didn't have the expensive video games and computers, so we relied on what nature provided for us. For example, we spent hours clinging to the barren, granite cliffs in an attempt to pry away a few loose rocks that would send an avalanche into the sea, and our favourite pastime was catching conners and tom cods* off the stage head.* I have since wondered how we escaped from being swept into the sea with the foundering stones or if the tom cod felt it when we caught it on a bare hook, popped out its eyes to use as bait to entice the more cunning conner, and then threw the poor blind creature back into the water. I have also wondered if the flatfish died soon after we pinned it to the ocean bottom with a sharpened pole so as to feel the pole quiver in our grasp. We were no less sadistic to the sculpin, the thorny scavenger of the sea who was not welcomed on our hooks. In an act of vengeance, we devised an elaborate plan to subject the innocent creature to a horrible death. You see, if one were to pat the belly of a sculpin when it is taken from the water, the poor brute will gulp air and blow up. This very fact created much, so called, sport for us because each sculpin caught was whipped into a bloated state and released to float belly up, atop of the water, while hopelessly struggling to turn itself over to dive. Then, the more conscious-minded among us attempted to release the air by taking pot shots at the swimming target with BB guns. Most times, however, we missed or the guns were not powerful enough to penetrate the thick skin of the gut, and the sculpin swam out of our reach to be snatched up by a hungry seagull.

Being a fishing nation, it was only natural, I suppose, that various species of fish became the object of our play. In early summer when the caplin scull* came, the beaches became a playground for young and old. The little fish were collected in the millions to be fried fresh, to be pickled or smoked for winter provisions, and to be used as fertilizer for the potato gardens. We

---

*A young cod fish that swims close to shore.
*The part of the fishing stage that is built out over the water and is used to land and clean fish.
*A time when the caplin roll on the beaches in the thousands to spawn. This occurs annually around the end of June.

young laddioes* searched among the beached multitudes and collected the females that were plump with spawn. Holding the little fish firmly in one's fist and squeezing it hard sent a jet of caviar twenty-feet into the air. We used these as weapons against the girls. I remember one time I caught Queenie Marsh on her way to church. Unaware of the danger that was lurking nearby, she went tripping along with her hymn book tucked under her arm while her long silky hair was blowing in the wind. I inconspicuously sneaked up behind her, pulled out two pregnant pistols and let her have it with both barrels. The seedy substance stuck to her hair like holy bread to the roof of the mouth. The church was warm that morning and the blue arse flies had awakened after a winter of hibernation. They descended on poor Queenie and almost lugged her away. Queenie is living on the mainland now. I saw her two years ago at a "come home year" event. She remembered me well and said, "We used to have some fun when we were growing up." I guess Queenie is not into video games.

Now, because I'm the Schoolmaster and getting up in years, many ask, "how can you stand it with the young crowd being the way they are today?" This is asked with such conviction that I almost feel guilty telling them that my job is easier now than it was when I started years ago. As a matter of fact, the worst thing to have happened at the Roaring Cove School in the past number of years was when young Susan Rodgers stole the bobbin off the sewing machine in the home economics room. If I compare this to when the flatulence four were in school, it is like comparing the two World Wars to a day of berry picking.

The flatulence four consisted of Alfie Lambert, Joe Stead, Art Pearce, and Bobby Johnson, and they were so named because each of them possessed an extraordinary fascination with farting. They sat in the back of the classroom and amused, distracted and terrorized the other students with their sounds and smells. If I separated them, it only made matters worse because the entire room then became a battlefield of exploding bombs and dispersing gas.

---

*A mischievous young boy.

Alfie Lambert was the ringleader of the group. His motto was, wherever you may be, let your wind go free 'cause the nipping of wind was the killing of me. This he lived by and encouraged others to do the same. He was notorious for letting one drop and blaming it on some little girl, but his special talent in the area of flatulence, or gas passing, was an astute ability to classify and name particular types of anal actions. "That was a cabbage fart," he'd proudly announce, or he'd tag it with some other term like, a beano, a popper, a screecher, a hangover special, a misfire, a double smack, a sizzler, and the list went on. One day I was bending over his desk helping him with his school work; it was just before lunch and my stomach was rumbling and growling, calling out for food. Alfie looked up at me and said, "Sir, you're havin' upthroughmes."

"I am having what?"

"Upthroughmes, sir," he repeated with a giggle which drew snickers from the rest of the class.

"And what exactly is an upthroughme?" I asked, knowing full well that Alfie had dangled the bait and I had taken it.

"It's a windy puff that goes up through your body instead of down through to your…"

"That's enough, Alfie!" I snapped.

It was Alfie who nicknamed Art Pearce the crepitator because of his ability to rattle out quick and repetitive sounds. Art and his entire family were bean eaters, boiled beans, baked beans, stewed beans, and tin beans were very important parts of their diet. Beans contain a particular type of non-digestive sugar that, when mixed with the bacteria of the gut, creates large amounts of gas — in Art's case massive amounts. On average, a person produces about one half litre of flatus gas a day, or about fourteen rousers.* Art would rip out that many in a single succession, while Alfie counted and named each one aloud. Thankfully, this type of gas is not particularly smelly, just annoyingly noisy.

Joe Stead was the smelly one or the stink bomb as Alfie referred to him. It was Joe who inflated the heating bill in our school

*To vigorously break wind.

because he made it necessary for the windows to be perpetually opened. Again it was Art's diet that gave him this distinction. The odour in flatus gas comes from a hydrogen sulfide present in foods, therefore, the more sulfur in the diet the more smelly is the gas that is created. Foods like eggs, cabbage, and meats are notorious for this, and Joe's father kept cows and hens, and a pork and cabbage supper was the family's favourite meal. The result was that Joe could cause the paint on the walls to peel.

The fourth member of the flatulence four, Bobby Johnson, was the most quiet but the most dangerous. Apparently, people who swallow a lot of air break wind more. Bobby, who stutters, frequently gulped in air when he was trying to get something out. This caused his stomach to bloat like a landed sculpin. A chemical reaction in the stomach produces this air into a gas consisting of nitrogen, carbon dioxide, hydrogen, and, in 30 percent of people, methane. Now, methane is highly flammable, and Bobby was in this 30 percent. This boosted Bobby to the ranks of stardom and he was frequently called upon to "light one." Delighted with the attention, Bobby would oblige with a spectacular fireworks display. If I were absent from the room, the lights were turned out, the curtains were drawn, Bobby contorted himself, and catapulted a blue flame that dispersed itself around him like gasoline set alight on water. This is why Bobby was dangerous — igniting flatus gas is a dangerous practice and, out of concern for Bobby, I spoke to Dr. Templeman about it. He assured me that the behaviour could result in flames backing up into the colon, and it was indeed a most hazardous stunt. Luckily, Bobby did not have this happen to him but he did destroy several school uniforms by scorching the backside on several pairs of flannel pants. As a matter of fact, I heard from a good source that Bobby is still lighting them. Apparently, on a dare from Alfie, Bobby lit one in church when Reverend King was praying for Thumb-On-Wrench Swyers' recovery.

It would have been a pertinent time for the good Reverend to have said a special prayer about inappropriate behaviour and reckless ways and requested that the flock be more diligent when tending to the congregation.

Foreign Cuisine

"The moon was beginning to walk on the still sea before the elder men came aft...Harvey followed Penn and sat down before a tin pan of cods' tongues and sounds, mixed with scraps of pork and fried potato, a loaf of hot bread, and some black and powerful coffee." Rudyard Kipling – Captains Courageous

Everyone in Roaring Cove knows that Uncle Mark White has an awful weak stomach and is very particular about what he eats. He likes, what we refer to as, the old-fashioned, rough grub – salt meat and cabbage, fish and brewis* and fish and spuds, laced with scrunchions,* pea soup with soggy dumplings, a salt-water duck or a turr* – that sort of thing. He is very reluctant to try anything different and most selective about who prepares his food. When the church has its fundraising suppers and the women contribute boilers of soup, he will specifically ask for Aunt Daisy Snelgrove's, claiming that he likes her soup the best. I know, though, it is because he knows that Aunt Daisy is super clean. He refuses to buy bakeapples from the Kellop Harbour crowd because he heard that they shuck them with their teeth, and one time he found a hair in a cold plate he bought from the fire department and he was sick for a week.

"God only knows whose head it came from," he said. "Perhaps Jonas Pickett's"

Aunt Mae claims that Uncle Mark is tabbety* and hard to cook for; and recently, they had a falling out because Uncle Mark was refusing to accept an invitation to dinner.

It all started back in the fall when Dr. Templeman decided, for the first time in his life, to take an extended holiday and spend his

---

*Hard tact or a hard biscuit soaked overnight and briefly boiled and served, instead of vegetables, particularly with fish.
*Tiny pieces of fatback pork that are fried until crispy and served over fish.
*A sea bird that is hunted for food.
*To be particular over food.

winter in a warmer climate, and Aunt Daisy and Uncle Al decided to spend the winter with their only daughter on the mainland. Although Dr. Templeman allowed that, if he had known Aunt Daisy was going to be away all winter, it would have been holiday enough for him. However, the situation worked out well because Aunt Daisy rented her house to Dr. Templeman's replacement. She was thrilled that the house would not need to be barred up, and she immediately started cleaning and scrubbing to make sure everything was clean for the young doctor and his wife. Every pot, pan and dish was scoured; the walls, floors and ceilings were washed down; the bedclothes, curtains, and mats were soaked. Everything was immaculate, and Aunt Daisy was satisfied with the condition of her house. Nevertheless, there was one thing that bothered her. The thought of complete strangers using her most personal items sent her hypochondria into the danger zone.

She consulted Dr. Templeman. "I understand they're coming from overseas." she stated.

"That's correct, Aunt Daisy," Dr. Templeman responded.

"I s'pose they wouldn't have some rare disease, would they?"

"No, Aunt Daisy."

"Are they clean, doctor?"

"Yes, Aunt Daisy."

Aunt Daisy was not satisfied. She promptly, removed her personal dishes from the cupboard and locked them in the hutch, and her private bedclothes were packed in a cardboard box and tucked away in the attic. She took her chamber pot from underneath her bed and put it away in the hall closet. She claimed this was done, not for hygienic reasons, but for safety reasons — Aunt Daisy's pot was handed down from her grandmother and was of great sentimental value — and besides, fancy, porcelain chamber pots are not easily found today.

Dr. and Mrs. Ismah came from India. They were a delightful couple who took good care of Aunt Daisy's house and made good neighbours. Uncle Mark and Aunt Mae befriended them like they do all newcomers and introduced them to the Roaring Cove ways

— especially our food. Aunt Mae cooked up the traditional stuff for them, and Uncle Mark embellished each meal with a story. The young couple were entertained with fishing and hunting adventures and were instructed how to make salt fish, to pickle cabbage, to bottle wild game, and to smoke salmon. The newcomers were enthralled with the hospitality and were eager to return it. Nevertheless, Uncle Mark wanted no part of it; this was the dinner invitation that he was refusing to accept.

"I'm going with or without you, Mark!" I heard Aunt Mae say as I entered their kitchen. The tone of her voice told me that something was brewing.

"What's going on? Where are ya goin', Aunt Mae? Gonna leave Uncle Mark after all of these years?" I asked, trying to make light of the fact that I had walked in on them unannounced.

"'Tis Mark being stubborn again," Aunt Mae responded.

Uncle Mark looked embarrassed, and he fumbled with the wood in the wood box before he spoke. "Mae is makin' a big deal over nothin'," he said. "She wants to go over to Dr. Ismah's for dinner, and I don't want to go."

"Why not?" I asked. "We're invited too, and I'm lookin' forward to it. That's why I came in — I figured you'd be invited."

"Might be all right for you, Schoolmaster — you'd eat anything," Uncle Mark replied, "but I don't think I'd like their kind of food."

It was easy to see that Aunt Mae was worked up, and she shot back. "I don't mind you, Mark. You're like a youngster over a bit a grub, you are. You got to have everything cooked just so and you're not willing to try anything you weren't raised on."

"But their grub is different and I don't like it."

"How do you know if you've never had it?" Aunt Mae asked.

"I knows I don't like it 'cause I smells it on their clothes."

"Very good, then," Aunt Mae continued, "that's what I'll tell them when I go over. I'll say, 'Mark didn't come because he don't like the smell of your clothes.'"

"But I'd only offend them good people if I went to dinner and didn't eat their food," Uncle Mark reasoned.

"I think you'll doubly offend them if you don't go at all," I commented.

"You think so?" he said.

"I'm sure of it," I responded.

Uncle Mark had begun to soften and Aunt Mae and I went to work on him. Before I left, he had agreed to consider it — if I could find out what they would be serving.

The next time I saw Dr. Ismah relaxing on Aunt Daisy's front bridge, as he liked to do, I made a casual visit and we engaged in friendly conversation. He reminded me about our dinner plans and mentioned that he was looking forward to it because Mrs. Ismah was preparing her speciality, curried lamb and chicken.

"They're serving chicken and lamb," I told Uncle Mark. I left out the curry part.

"Well, that don't sound too bad," he responded. "I've eaten enough chicken in me day, and I don't mind a bit of mutton every now and then. I think I'll give it a try."

We decided to arrive together; so, on the night of the dinner, my wife and I arrived at Uncle Mark's around six o'clock. He and Aunt Mae were sitting on the daybed waiting for us. They were dressed in their Sunday best, and they somewhat resembled two figures atop of a wedding cake.

"We'll wait a little bit," said Uncle Mark. "We don't want to seem too anxious."

"Well, I'm not waitin' much longer," Aunt Mae responded. "I'm starved. I haven't eaten all day."

It was a beautiful fall evening, the air was still and cool, and a gorgeous full moon was poking above the eastern hills and reflecting on the harbour. When we opened Aunt Daisy's gate, the smell of curry and turmeric filled the front garden. Uncle Mark began sniffing at the sky like a black bear downwind of a barbecue.

"What's that queer smell?" he asked.

Aunt Mae quickly grabbed him by the sleeve and dragged him up the front steps. "Nothin'!" she snapped, "and Mark, you had better eat everything that's put on your plate, or I won't cook another thing for a month."

The Ismahs cheerily greeted us at the door, and we were led into Aunt Daisy's parlour. I immediately noticed that a different fragrance permeated the room, and Uncle Mark began to sniff the air again. "That's a nice smell," he said, "smells just like oakum."

Then I noticed two incense sticks burning on each end table and I pointed to them.

"Is that dope?" Uncle Mark asked in a barely audible voice.

"Incense," my wife murmured.

"I don't know if Aunt Daisy would approve of smokin' up the place like that," Aunt Mae whispered.

Dr. Ismah joined us with wine and drinks. Uncle Mark had a couple good shots of rum and was feeling relaxed by the time he went to the dinner table. When we entered the kitchen, the strong smell of spices was again present. The table was beautifully decorated with burning candles and matching napkins, but the dishes and cutlery were of different kinds and sizes. The counter area was cluttered with different pots, pans and dippers. It was obvious that Aunt Daisy had removed her good kitchenware and poor Mrs. Ismah had to be creative to find enough utensils to serve us dinner.

Firstly, she served an appetizer. I have no idea what it was called, but it was extremely delicious. It was a wide tubular noodle stuffed with some kind of minced meat, and it was covered in clear broth. This she served in saucers.

"Well…well…'tis squid," said Uncle Mark, and he devoured the entire thing as if he had been eating it every day of his life.

The main meal, consisting of several items, was placed on the table for us to help ourselves. Mrs. Ismah named each of the dishes, but the names were foreign to me and I understood the words chicken and lamb only. She explained that the food was prepared by the degree of spice added and she pointed out which dishes were mild and which were hot. The doctor started off and spooned a sample of each into his plate. The rest of us followed suit. When it came Uncle Mark's turn, he just sat dazed, and looked from one item to the other. Finally, Aunt Mae took his plate and sparingly served him a little of each item.

I started with the mildest of the dishes. The flavour of curry was predominate, and each serving was truly delicious, but, by the time I got to the hottest, beads of sweat were breaking out on the top of my head.

I looked at Uncle Mark. He was sitting there staring at his plate, unsure of where to begin. Suddenly, Aunt Mae elbowed him in the ribs and gave him her raised eyebrow look, and he started in. He drove his fork into the hot curried lamb and lifted it to his lips. Instinctively, he blew his breath on it like a child attempting to cool off hot porridge. Then he popped it into his mouth. His eyes widened, his jaw fell, and water welled up in his eyes. He hyperventilated and waved his hand in front of his mouth before swallowing hard.

"Too hot for you, Uncle Mark?" the doctor asked grinning slightly.

"No 'tis good," Uncle Mark answered reaching for the water jug.

With great caution Uncle Mark continued to pick away at his food, taking tiny portions and washing it down with water. His neck turned red and the colour rose to the tips of his ears, but he remained silent and bravely picked away at his meal.

Suddenly, Mrs. Ismah jumped up. "Oh, my!" she said. "I forgot the rice." She went to the stove, pulled open the oven door and removed a large pot of rice. She placed it, smack dab, in the middle of the table and encouraged us to help ourselves. I looked at the bowl. I looked the second time. I made eye contact with my wife, and the look on her face confirmed what I already knew. There was no mistaking it; it was Aunt Daisy's porcelain chamber pot. Immediately, Aunt Mae, began spooning the rice into her plate and didn't seem to notice anything unusual. Uncle Mark was staring at her with a look of pure horror. He looked at me questioningly. I quickly glanced away.

Shortly, though, Mrs. Ismah went to the stove for something, and the doctor went to get a bottle of wine. Uncle Mark kicked me under the table and caught my attention. He nodded his head at the rice bowl. "Is that Aunt Daisy's piss pot?" he asked under his breath.

"No," I lied, and like a young boy in church I began to giggle.

"What's that yellow stuff around the rim?" he whispered.

"Curry," I mouthed.

"My, this rice is lovely, Mrs. Ismah," Aunt Mae interjected smacking her lips.

"Thank you," she responded politely.

Uncle Mark gulped hard, cupped his hand over his mouth, and headed for the bathroom.

"Is he ill?" the good doctor asked with concern.

"Naw, that's just Mark. I dare say he finds the food a bit too hot," Aunt Mae responded while continuing to chew on her food.

We were almost finished when Uncle Mark returned to the table; he was holding his stomach and he had lost all of his colour.

"If you find the food too hot, Uncle Mark," Dr. Ismah said, "you can tone it down with some rice.

"No...no...thank you...I'm a potato man."